Josh McDowell's Guide to Understanding Your Bible

Josh McDowell's Guide to Understanding Your Bible

A Simple, Step-by-Step Method
for Effective Bible Study
and Life Application

Josh McDowell

JOSH MCDOWELL'S GUIDE TO UNDERSTANDING YOUR BIBLE
Copyright ©1982, 2006 by Josh D. McDowell

Cover Design: Terry Dugan

ALL RIGHTS RESERVED
Scripture quotations are taken from the Holy Bible, New Living Translation, copyright © 1996, 2004. Used by permission of Tyndale House Publishers, Inc., Wheaton, Illinois 60189. All rights reserved. Scripture quotations marked NASB are taken from the New American Standard Bible®, copyright © 1960, 1962, 1963, 1968, 1971, 1972, 1973, 1975, 1977, 1995 by The Lockman Foundation. Used by permission. Scripture quotations marked GWT are taken from GOD'S WORD® Translation, copyright ©1995 by God's Word to the Nations. Used by permission. All rights reserved.

No part of this publication may be reproduced, stored in a retrieval system, or transmitted in any form or by any means—electronic, mechanical, photocopying, recording, or otherwise—without prior written permission.

Editorial assistance provided by The Livingstone Corporation (www.livingstonecorp.com). Project staff includes Linda Taylor and Mary Larsen.

Published by Green Key Books
2514 Aloha Place
Holiday, Florida 34691

Library of Congress Cataloging-in-Publication Data

McDowell, Josh.
  Guide to understanding your Bible : a simple, step-by-step method for effective Bible study and life application / Josh McDowell.
    p. cm.
  ISBN 1-932587-65-9 (alk. paper)
  1. Bible—Study and teaching. I. Title.
  BS600.3.M33 2006
  220.071--dc22
                                      2006020404

Printed in the United States of America.

06 07 08 09 5 4 3 2 1

Contents

Chapter 1. Why Study the Bible? • 7
Chapter 2. Getting the Big Picture • 19

Step One: How to "See It." A Guide to Observation
Chapter 3. Ask the Right Questions • 35
Chapter 4. Dig Deeper • 49
Chapter 5. See How It Works • 61

Step Two: How to "Know It." A Guide to Interpretation
Chapter 6. Interpretation—Find the True Meaning • 73
Chapter 7. Let the Bible Interpret for You • 81
Chapter 8. Search Outside the Bible • 95
Chapter 9. Your Final Product • 109

Step Three: How to "Do It." A Guide to Application
Chapter 10. Principles of Application • 123
Chapter 11. Need-Driven Bible Study • 141
Chapter 12. You Can Do It • 153

Appendices
Appendix A: Bonus Resources • 159
Appendix B: Paraphrasing, Topical Study and
 Biographical Study • 161
Appendix C: True Foundations • 171

Chapter 1: Why Study the Bible?
Making God's Truth Your Own

If you are like me, you have experienced numerous instances in which you wanted to know the Bible well enough that passages you needed would spring instantly to mind. Perhaps you needed insight into a problem, guidance for an important decision, wisdom to help a friend or seeker, or maybe you simply needed inspiration to face the day.

You may think, *Yes, I want that kind of Bible knowledge, but it's just not possible for me. I can't even remember what I had for lunch yesterday, much less some obscure passage from the book of Habakkuk.* I understand your thinking because I once thought the same way. But not any more. I have developed a method of Bible study that has given me a tremendous storehouse of Bible knowledge that I can tap into at will. I can recall countless biblical passages and principles in situations where I can't lay my hands on a Bible, such as when driving a car.

If you think this method must involve hours and hours of Scripture memorization, let me put your mind at ease. I think Scripture memorization is valuable, and I recommend it. But that's not what this book is about. It is not a method of training you to absorb *Scripture* at all, but rather one designed to help you absorb the *content* of Scripture in a way so simple and straightforward that you will actually enjoy it. Now, when I say "simple" I don't mean there's no work involved. By "simple" I mean that my method is not complicated or hard to understand. Nothing worthwhile comes without effort. But if you invest the effort, I feel sure that you will experience the same exhilaration I felt as the knowledge of God's Word grew in my heart and became a part of me. David the psalmist put it beautifully: "The commandments of the LORD are right, bringing joy to the heart" (Psalm 19:8).

I'm sure I don't need to convince you of the importance of the Bible. If you did not believe in its value and its truth, you would not have picked up this book. With so many study Bibles on the market, however, and with so much Bible computer software and online resources available, you may wonder why a book on understanding your Bible is necessary. Many of these resources give you the kind of introductory information to each book of the Bible that I will teach you to learn for yourself in the following pages. Why not simply read all about the meaning, writing, background, and message of the book of Isaiah in a study Bible instead of digging it out for yourself?

Well, that "digging it out for yourself" is the key. Your knowledge needs to be your own—deeply rooted in your heart and personal to you. We all understand that an inherited, secondhand faith is seldom meaningful or strong. Though you may have been raised in the church by godly parents or came to the Lord at the persuasion of a friend, you must at some point come to know the truth for yourself and make your beliefs personally yours. The truth in your heart must be more than a set of propositions you accept passively from your parents or teachers. Similarly, the meaning of the Bible will be richer and more deeply imbedded if you build the foundations for your knowledge in your own heart instead of passively adopting the work of others.

Christians today are sometimes conditioned to be taught from the Scriptures but not to dig out the truths for themselves. The process of finding truth for yourself leads to greater personal conviction. Sixteenth-century monk Martin Luther felt this conviction so strongly that he translated the Bible into German, the language of the people. The same conviction spurred Cameron Townsend to start the work of Wycliffe Bible Translators, enabling people all over the world to have Bibles in their own language for personal study. Wycliffe translator Chet Bitterman held this conviction so tightly that he was willing to give his life for it.

I have nothing against study Bibles, computer software, or online Bible resources. I recommend them. I am grateful for them. I even use them. In this book I will direct you to such resources and show you how I use some of them. But I urge students to use these resources to build a personal knowledge of the Bible with their own hands rather than depending on them as their primary repository of knowledge to which they turn every time they need answers. The idea is to use these resources to fill your own mind rather than depend on them as your external source of knowledge that you can plug into whenever necessary.

The Importance of Discipline

Studying the Word of God is much like walking in the Spirit. It is a steady, day-to-day growth process. The way is uneven and you will encounter various moods as you travel. On some days you will seem to be on the mountaintop. Everything you read and study will be exhilarating and the switches of your mind will click on. On other days you will trudge though a valley. The process will seem like drudgery and your mind will not focus on the task. The important thing is to ignore the moods and keep walking. Consistency will pay off.

Many people seem to think the truths of the Bible will leap out at them the moment they open the book. In this day of instant gratification, that's what we often expect. We want the results in our hands day before yesterday. But God doesn't work that way. He is committed to the process as well as to the product because he knows that the former guarantees the latter. That is always his way. He spent forty years preparing Moses, three years preparing Paul, and fifteen years preparing Joseph. Why should we get in a rush?

Bible study involves time, commitment, and application. Yet so does mathematics, biochemistry, playing the piano, building a house, or flying a plane. Nothing worthwhile comes without effort and dedication. You will dedicate yourself to something, even if it's by default. Some people dedicate themselves to their own leisure in front of the television. They become experts at spelling words on *Wheel of Fortune*, at trivia questions on *Jeopardy*, or the intricacies of the characters' lives on their favorite soap opera. Isn't a few hours of work learning the Bible much more rewarding than dulling one's mind with a passive electronic diet of inanity?

The Goals of This Study

Our ultimate goal in understanding the Bible is not *interpretation* but *application*. We don't seek more head knowledge for its own sake, but rather we desire to conform our lives and ministries as close as possible to the image of Jesus Christ. The goal is not merely to *know* more, but to *learn* more of God's will for our lives. The goal is to be able to *apply* God's Word to our daily lives and to display God's nature to others.

The Three Commitments

To accomplish these goals, you must make three commitments. *First, you must direct your will.* How serious are you about studying God's Word and growing as a Christian? How strong is your longing to become conformed to the image of Christ? As Christ himself prayed, "And this is the way to have eternal life—to know you, the only true God, and Jesus Christ, the one you sent to earth" (John 17:3).

Second, you must walk in the Spirit. As the apostle Paul tells us in Ephesians 5:18, "Be filled with the Holy Spirit." Unless you open yourself to God's Holy Spirit, he cannot teach you. A mere cold and mechanical study of the Bible will give you facts but not discernment or wisdom. The information may lodge in your head, but the book will not open to you and flood your life unless you submit to the leading and illumination the Holy Spirit will give you. Walking in the Spirit means to examine every area of your life, ridding each area of anything contrary to God's will, and cleansing yourself by confessing any known sin. The apostle John tells us, "If we confess our sins to him, he is faithful and just to forgive us our sins and to cleanse us from all wickedness" (1 John 1:9). Ask the Holy Spirit to fill you—to control and empower you day by day.

Third, you must live in the Word. I like to call it "logging time" in the Word. Unless you spend time reading the Bible seriously, you cannot grow in your understanding of it no matter how much information you process in the exercises I will show you in this book. The Bible itself, not merely study about the Bible, is the key to understanding.

Donald Grey Barnhouse, a former pastor of the Tenth Presbyterian Church in Philadelphia, was traveling by train and reading his Bible. A young student seated across the aisle looked up from his news magazine and recognized the imminent churchman. After a while, he worked up the nerve to ask, "Dr. Barnhouse, how can I be a man of the Word and know the Bible like you?" The pastor looked at the student's stack of reading material and replied, "Son, as long as you read those magazines more than you read this Book, you will know more about those magazines than you know about this Book."

Dr. Barnhouse was not denying the importance of knowing our culture; he was referring to priorities. What comes first? What do you read most? Is the Bible a high priority in your life?

The Purpose

The purpose of this book is not to have you master the Word, but to have the Word master you. Head knowledge of the Bible is worthless unless it leads to a complete transformation of your life. As Paul said in Romans 12:2,

> *Don't copy the behavior and customs of this world, but let God transform you into a new person by changing the way you think. Then you will learn to know God's will for you, which is good and pleasing and perfect.*

The idea of Bible study is to get you in the mode of thinking like Christ. As you begin to think like Christ, you begin to act like Christ. And perhaps today, more than any other time in American history, we have an urgent need for people to model Christ to our society.

More than likely, you accept the Bible as true and inspired. Yet think how different that is from the prevailing postmodern mindset of our young people. You claim to have an exclusive truth—a truth that negates all other truth claims. And that truth is universal and absolute—the truth for all people at all times in all places. You claim that truth is recorded in a book. All of these claims run head-on into the prevailing philosophy that there is no absolute truth—that all truth claims are equal. Those who hold this philosophy will not believe your book. To show them the truth about Christ, you will need to model it. You will need to show them a way of living that makes their mouths water. You will need to study *the* book, come to know the Person it tells of, model your life after his, and give your peers the ultimate demonstration of love by displaying and passing on the love of Christ. That is the ultimate importance of Bible study. You take the truth of the book into yourself, make it your own, and bring it alive in your own life for others to see.

So it's not about rules. God doesn't want us to study the Bible just to learn the laws of the Christian life or gain inspiration to live better. When you open yourself to the Bible, you open a door to his heart—a way to know him for who he is. And his invitation to know him for who he is brings with it the power to live like him (2 Peter 1:3–4). When the Word takes hold in your heart, your life and your words will testify of God's reality to the world. Because God is in you, you show God to others.

God chose us to be part of his family because this brings him great pleasure. He chose us to become like him because this is our place in his master plan from the beginning. He chose us to reflect him to others because this is his path for bringing blessing to the world. And without the Word of God in our heart we would be without an accurate revelation of God, unable to know him for who he is. That is the significance of the Bible to each one of us and to our everyday lives. God's Word is the perfect lens to see God's person and our purpose, which is to reflect his divine nature.

In this book you will learn one approach to Bible study. If you apply yourself, you will learn the essence of the Bible inside out and know it better than you know your best friend. You will never again open your Bible without learning something. No doubt you have marveled at pastors or teachers who find insights you never thought of in passages you've read many times. And you wonder, "How did he see that?" If you diligently follow my study plan, you will begin to see this kind of thing yourself. You will see fresh meanings in familiar passages. Bible parallels and applications will pop up unbidden in all situations. You may want to show love to your wife or husband, boyfriend or girlfriend, and *voila!* You suddenly remember a principle about biblical love. You will turn a boring, bogged-down Bible study into an electrifying event. Every experience will be bathed in new light—God's light shining through the pages of the Bible and through the presence of his Holy Spirit in your life.

The Plan

It may seem that I am making Bible study too complicated. Why not just read the Bible and meditate, allowing the Holy Spirit to give us the insights we need? Well, if we were perfect creatures, such an approach might work; however, in this fallen world where dangers threaten our understanding, we need a little more structure to be sure our study guides us to what God is really saying.

The dangers of approaching Bible study haphazardly are many and great. One danger is that we will fail to understand a passage correctly because we simply do not observe carefully what it really says. Another danger is that of misunderstanding because we have only partial information on the subject we are studying. Often the Bible will clarify itself if we only know where to find related passages of Scripture. Another danger is that of studying a passage without relating it to its context. The meaning of any verse will be invariably influenced by the verses preceding and following it. The Bible study method you are about to learn will help you to avoid these dangers.

Here is how we will proceed. First, I will walk you through my Bible study method step-by-step, showing you exactly how it works. After the overview, I will then show you how to apply your study to your life.

In my past, I rebuilt old cars and sold them. Before I started tearing an engine apart, I wanted to see it intact first. I wanted to know how the engine should look before I dismantled it into hundreds of little pieces. With that overall picture in mind, I could then reassemble the engine because I understood it in its wholeness. That, in a nutshell, explains the overarching plan of my Bible study method. At the beginning we will put on our wide-angle lens, getting a clear view of the big picture. Then we will take it apart. We will move in with a microscope to see all the little pieces and learn how they add up to the whole.

We will start with a Bible book, using it as our model for study, go from there to the individual chapters, then to the paragraphs, the verses, the phrases, and finally to the words. Our example book will be the gospel of John, especially chapters 3 and 4. We will reach out into other passages, but these two will be our focus. I chose John because I believe it is easy to learn and lends itself to this type of study. It almost seems that the apostle had Bible study in mind when he wrote the book.

Here is an overview of how we will proceed.

Charting

I will teach you how to construct several charts designed to capture what you learn as you study. These charts are not your final material; they are preparatory notes designed for information capture—a handy means of recording the information you glean as you work through the Bible study process. The charts will become your source of information for preparing final outlines of the material after you have recorded it and organized it.

The first of these charts is a Title Chart enabling you to keep what you learn organized and in context. The Title Chart will begin with the big picture and descend into the details as follows:

```
The Book
      Chapters
            Paragraphs
                  Verse
                        Phrases
                              Words
```

The Title Chart will keep the big picture before you as you work the details. With the Title Chart in place, we will move into the three basic steps of Bible study. As we proceed through these steps, I will introduce a new chart with each step to help you organize your preliminary capture of information so you will have it at hand when you construct your final outline. (See Appendix A on page 159 for instructions on downloading Bonus Resources, a free supplement with printable charts and additional samples.)

Three Major Steps of Bible Study

See It

This step teaches you the principle of observation, to ask of a passage, "What do I see here?" The goal is to learn to see exactly what the passage really says—to see past the surface and discover deeper truths that are embedded but often overlooked in superficial readings.

Know It
This step teaches the principle of interpretation. Here we ask the question, "What does it mean?" In this step, we want not only to be sure we see all that's being said, we want to understand it.

Do It
This is my term for application. In this step, we reach the ultimate goal of Bible study and ask, "What does it mean to me?" or more pointedly, "How does this apply to me?" You must know what a passage means and how it applies before you can adopt it into your life. And that application to your life is what the whole process is really about—not merely to learn it but to *do it*.

Practice, Practice, Practice

A young man rushed frantically down a street in New York City, obviously lost. As he approached a corner a taxi stopped and let out the distinguished Artur Rubenstein, one of the twentieth century's musical virtuosos. The desperate young man did not recognize the great pianist. He ran up to him and asked, "Sir, can you tell me how to get to Carnegie Hall?" Rubenstein answered, "Yes. Practice, practice, practice."

Practice is also the key to studying the Bible. You can't get there without effort. My study method is not hard in the sense that it's complicated or difficult to understand. But there's no way around it; Bible study does require work. To me, however, the work is fascinating. The process of discovery is its own reward because the uncovering of new information is like solving a mystery.

The beauty of this method is that it makes no specific time requirements of you. You will benefit from thirty minutes of study or from three hours, and the benefits will be proportional to the time investment. Think of Bible study in this way: It's not an academic course that you take once and then you're done with it. What you will learn here is a way of study that you will be able to use for the rest of your life, every time you open your Bible. It's a simple, organized approach to learning God's truth that you can use from now on. So, this book will introduce you to the method, and for the rest of your life you can put it into practice, practice, practice.

Assignment

1. Read Psalm 19:7–11 and list three reasons why studying the Bible is good for you personally.
2. Read John 3 and 4 three times in one sitting.

Chapter 2: Getting the Big Picture
Making a Title Chart

You've seen those amazing zoom shots on television or the internet that open by showing the entire world from outer space. Then the camera moves in. As the world gets closer, North America fills the screen, then the United States, and then New England. Still the camera moves in until you are looking down on the distant buildings of a city. The camera moves closer yet until you can see the streets with cars moving on them and people walking on the sidewalks. The camera aims at a particular building, then at a particular window and zooms inside. Moving continuously, it focuses on a single desk, then on a paper resting on that desk, and it moves in and stops, allowing you to read the words on that paper.

It's a marvel to me how state-of-the-art computer graphics give us a single, seamless zoom shot that brings us from deep space to a few inches above a paper on a desk. It illustrates the process we are about to begin in this chapter. We will start, so to speak, in "outer space." That is, in this chapter our camera will focus on the big picture. We will zoom in closer as the book proceeds.

The Title Chart

Our device for viewing the big picture will not be a camera, but a chart, which we will call the "Title Chart." To get an idea of the value of a Title Chart, consider the following illustration:

You are just getting into bed after a hard day when the phone rings. Your daughter is on the line, calling from her college dorm. After a few minutes of chat, she explains the purpose of her call. "Dad," she says, "I've been talking to my roommate about spiritual things, and she is having trouble understanding the resurrection of

Jesus. Can you give me a few Scripture passages to discuss with her?" How many passages could you give her in that instant? If you answer "few" or "none," you will find the Title Chart to be a highly useful tool in turning that response around.

A Title Chart will help you recall what is in a given chapter of a given book of the Bible. Your preparation and study of the chart will fix this kind of knowledge in your mind without the special effort of memorizing. In addition to revealing the whole book at a glance, the chart will give you the overall theme of the book. It will provide you with a sort of lattice into which the laces of your study and research can weave themselves as you add to your knowledge. The Title Chart makes a Bible book much easier to remember—and easier to teach.

As you probably know, in today's translations of the Bible you can get all this information easily without making a Title Chart. Most translations now break down chapters of the Bible into paragraphs with subheadings giving you the essential content of that paragraph. You may wonder why you should bother with a chart since this information is already available. I will say at this point that these Title Charts are optional to my Bible study method. If your Bible study time is severely limited, or if your goal is personal study only and not teaching, you may prefer to skip the Title Chart process. The meat of my method begins with the observation stage. As I said above, charting will drive the content of chapters home in your mind and get you inside the content. But if you are unable to do the Title Charts, you may choose to skip over them and go directly to the observation step.

Title Chart Preparation

Before you do anything else, I urge you to stop and spend a moment in prayer. You should always begin any study of the Bible by asking the Lord for his guidance and insight. Your prayer can be something like this: "Open my eyes that I may see and learn wonderful things from your Word and be willing to apply them."

Step 1: Read the Book

As I said in the previous chapter, we will use the gospel of John as our model for study, honing in on chapters 3 and 4 to teach my Bible study method and to prepare the charts. The first step before preparing a chart is to know your material. Before you begin the chart, you need to read the gospel of John at least twice—and more if possible. And you need to complete each reading in one sitting to insure comprehension and continuity.

Why multiple readings? Have you ever been to a movie the second time and marveled at how much you missed the first time? In the first viewing, or reading, you concentrate on the primary story. You focus on the big picture, trying to comprehend the overall movement of the material. You may miss subtleties, sub-points, side issues, or supporting information because of your single-minded concentration on "getting the big idea." Each subsequent reading fills in those gaps.

The great biblical expositor G. Campbell Morgan read a book thirty times before he attempted to study it. If you can read the gospel of John merely one-tenth that many times, you will be well on the path toward the kind of study I want to lead you through.

On your first reading, look for the book's stated purpose. It may be anywhere in the book—near the opening, in the middle, or at the end. In the book of John we find the stated purpose in chapter 20 verse 31: "But these are written so that you may continue to believe that Jesus is the Messiah, the Son of God, and that by believing in him you will have life by the power of his name." John makes it easy for us; he states his purpose simply and plainly. He wrote his book to convince people that Jesus is the Christ.

On your second reading, look for repeated phrases. For example, in Matthew's gospel he often uses the phrase, "When Jesus had finished." In Genesis we often find the phrase, "This is the history of," or "This is the account of." These repeated phrases will help you understand the development of the book's purpose.

On subsequent readings, look for the major divisions of the book. Books of the Bible may be divided into sections, with each section maintaining its own focus. Often these sections unify themselves into an overarching theme because they are parallel with each other. They are all of a given type. For example, the books of 1 and 2 Samuel have sections about different persons—Samuel, Saul, and David. Thus these books are organized around biographical themes. The big sections in Exodus organize themselves around geography—Israel in Egypt, at Sinai, and in the wilderness. The first eleven chapters of Genesis are organized around chronological events.

It's not as hard to discover these themes as you might think. In fact, every book in the Bible is organized around one of the five following themes:

1. Persons (1 and 2 Samuel, 1 and 2 Kings, Genesis 2–50)
2. Places (Acts, Joshua)
3. Events (the Gospels, Genesis 1–11)
4. Ideas (Romans, Proverbs)
5. Time (Luke, Revelation)

Step 2: Read about the Book

Next, I recommend that you read the introductory material on the gospel of John from a good study Bible. You may wonder why

I didn't send you to a study Bible first. After all, you can glean everything I recommended that you search for in step one from a study Bible. When I first began teaching my study method, few study Bibles were available and I urged students to dig out for themselves all the introductory material on a given Bible book. I still think the more you can find for yourself directly from Scripture, the better it will stick. But today study Bibles abound, published for every purpose and every need, and it's foolish not to take advantage of the excellent material available in them. Study Bibles will confirm or correct your own search of the Scripture and provide additional helpful information. Here are some of the items you can glean from a study Bible:

- A timeline of the book
- An introduction to the book
- The vital statistics of the book, including its purpose, the author, to whom it was written, the date written, the setting, the key verses, key places, key people, and other special features
- The megathemes of the book
- A map showing the key locations of the events of the book

In addition to study Bibles, many other fine Bible resources are available both on the Internet and in computer software. I will discuss the individual merits of these resources in a later chapter. The important point is to use these materials to help you gain your own knowledge and not as a crutch to lean on or a resource to run to because you don't want to put in the time to research these things for yourself.

Beginning the Title Chart

After you have read the gospel of John a few times and after you have familiarized yourself with the theme, divisions, and background of the book, you are ready to begin your first chart. You can use any method you choose to construct the chart. You may draw it by hand with pen and paper, or you may construct it on your computer. (See the sample on page 27, using John 1 as an example.)

Step 1: Chapter Titles

The first item to address is "Chapters."

Title Chart							
Chapters	1	2	3	4	5	6	7
Chapter Titles							

"Wait a minute, Josh," looking at the sample above, you may say, "these chapters are not titled." That's right. You must title them yourself. But before you begin the titling process, you must make a decision, which depends on what you hope to take away from the book. If your primary interest is the basic content of the book, you will title your chapters accordingly. If your interest is in the meaning or the theology of the book, your titles will reflect that focus. For example, if your focus is on content, you might choose as a title for John 11: "The Resurrection of Lazarus." If your focus is meaning or theology, you might choose something like: "Christ's Power over Death." In either case, the idea is the same. You want a title that summarizes the basic event or theme of the chapter—something that will help you recall the essential content of that chapter.

In many Bibles the publisher has already provided titles to the chapters. But if you want to gain expertise with the content yourself, I urge you to ignore these chapter titles (or better yet, work from a Bible edition that does not have them) and come up with your own. The exercise itself is an important part of the process of becoming familiar with the content of the Bible.

I want to point out one more thing before you begin: Remember that the authors themselves did not place the chapter divisions in the Bible. They wrote in a continuous stream of sentences with no breaks. Later scholars added chapter breaks for clarity and ease of study. Most of these chapter divisions fall in natural places, but some are unfortunate. So in your own study, you should feel free to adjust breaks if it helps you organize your material in a way that makes sense to you. You may occasionally feel a need to bring in a few verses from a previous chapter or reach a verse or two into the next to complete a thought. Don't hesitate. You are not desecrating the Word when you do this.

Make your chapter titles specific. If they are so general that they would fit any chapter in the book, you are not helping yourself learn the theme of a given chapter. When I recall specific chapter titles, I know immediately right where they fit into the book in relation to the other titles. The title gives me not only specific *content*, but also specific *context* because my title clearly differentiates that chapter from any other in the book. Think of your chapter titles as handles you can use to reach into a book and grab to pull out the content of a given chapter. It's also important to keep your chapter titles short so they will be easy to remember.

If you have a flair for humor, don't hesitate to use it in titling your chapters. One of my students titled John 4: "Well, Well," a clever pun based on the two main events of the chapter: the woman at the *well* and the nobleman's son made *well*. Another student titled John 9: "The Blind Man Sees More than the Pharisees," underscoring the idea that the Pharisees with all their theological training lacked the spiritual insight of the healed blind man. Be creative. Humor and creative titles are good memory tools.

Step 2: Paragraph Titles

After titling the chapters, we move on to titling each paragraph within each chapter. These paragraph titles fill the columns beneath the chapter titles. Not all Bibles use paragraph form, and obviously for this exercise you will need one that does. Be aware that even those translations that do use paragraphing do not all divide their chapters into paragraphs in the same way. For our purposes, that doesn't matter. Actually, as noted above, you should feel free to make your own paragraph divisions if yours make more sense to you than those in your Bible.

Your paragraph titles need to be short and to the point. They need not convey any detail at all. While you are getting started, you may want four to six words in your paragraph title because you lack the confidence to rely much on memory. But as you study and learn, it may take no more than two or three words to stimulate your recall. The whole purpose of titling paragraphs is to click the mouse in your memory that opens up all the information you know about that paragraph. Above each paragraph title you need to list the verses included in your paragraph.

To show you how the process works, let's look at John 1. As we work through this exercise, you may refer to the accompanying chart showing all my paragraph titles for this chapter. My chapter title for John 1 is "Jesus Recognized." This chapter title works well for me because it sets up a theme that I carry through in my paragraph titles. As you read on, you will see what I mean.

Getting the Big Picture

	Title Chart, John 1		
Chapters	Chapter 1	Chapter 2	Chapter 3
Chapter Titles	Jesus recognized		
Paragraph Titles	:1–5 Recognized as the Word :6–8 Recognized by John :9–13 Recognized by us :14–18 Recognized by His glory :19–28 Recognized by religious leaders :29–34 Recognized as Lamb of God :35–42 Recognized by Andrew :43–51 Recognized by Nathaniel		

The first paragraph in John 1 includes verses 1 through 5. In that paragraph, John introduces Jesus as the pre-existent God identified as the Word who is the Creator of all that exists. My title for that paragraph is: "Recognized as the Word." The next paragraph includes verses 6 through 8, in which we are introduced to John the Baptist who proclaimed the imminent coming of Jesus. My title for this paragraph is: "Recognized by John." My title for verses 9 through 13 is: "Recognized by Us," and for verses 14 through 18: "Recognized by His Glory." You can see the rest of the titles on the chart illustration, but I think you get the picture. All my paragraph titles reflect the theme I discovered in the chapter and stated in my chapter title—"Jesus Recognized."

This kind of consistent thematic repetition is a tremendous memory aid. The "recognized" theme appears in each paragraph heading giving my memory an initial push and keeping it on track. It's like making a necklace. Using the word "recognized" as the string, I can add the content of paragraphs to my memory pearl by pearl—recognized as the Word, recognized by John, recognized by us, recognized by his glory, etc. While this form works well for me, I fully realize that it may not work well for you. All minds process differently. It's important that you create paragraph titles that pull the right switches to trigger your memory.

In fact, you may want to invert the entire sequence of making this chart. Some people do. They find that they can understand the theme of a chapter and come up with a better chapter title if they start first with the paragraphs titles. The paragraph titles combine to suggest a chapter title. You should do whichever you find easiest and most helpful, and especially whichever helps you to lodge the information in your memory.

Now, just to prevent frustration, I will tell you that I don't always find such a neat, concise, completely unified theme that will give me a one-word string for my paragraph pearls. Sometimes the chapter subjects are so diverse that they can't be unified that simply. In fact, the next chapter of John is a case in point. In the first part of the chapter we have Jesus turning water into wine at the wedding feast in Cana. In the last part we see him cleansing the temple. If I were charting by theology instead of events, I might unify this chapter with a title something like, "Jesus Demonstrates His Authority." He demonstrated his authority over nature in the miracle, and over men in the temple cleansing. But since I am charting by events, I must stick to what the narrative tells me. Therefore, I came up with this extremely clever and astute title: "Wedding Wine and Temple Cleansed." Okay, that may not be clever or creative, but my point is that your title doesn't always have to be imaginative or concise; it just has to work to spark your memory.

Step 3: Key Words, Key Verses, and Background Material

At the bottom of your Title Chart, there should be columns for the *key verse* and the *key word* of that chapter. The key verse should be the one that comes closest to defining or summarizing the theme of the chapter. The key word may be one from that verse or one you choose that best captures the theme.

For example, the key verse of John chapter 1 might be the first verse, in which Jesus is recognized as God—the Word. The rest of the chapter defines and defends that assertion. The key word for the chapter would be—you guessed it—"recognized." For an example of how key words and verses look on a Title Chart, see the sample chart at the end of this chapter on page 31.

Key verses and key words are merely an additional extra to help you solidify the theme in your mind and help you remember.

It's the exclamation point at the end of the sentence—the cherry on top of the sundae.

After completing your Title Chart, you will find it helpful later to add a little information about the book now while it's fresh on your mind. Find some blank space somewhere on the chart—on the back if necessary—and add the following:

- The author
- The date the book was written
- Where it was written
- Key verse
- Key word
- Historical setting
- Geographical setting
- Any other pertinent information you find helpful or interesting

All of this information is readily available in Bible handbooks, Bible dictionaries, study Bibles, or commentaries. It's also available in Bible study computer software or online at such sites as Biblegateway.com.

Assignment

1. Read the book of John.
2. Read John 1 through 6 at least three times.
3. Construct your Title Chart following the instructions in this chapter.

Getting the Big Picture

Title Chart: Galatians, Student Sample*

Chapters	1	2	3	4	5	6
Chapter Titles	Paul's Auto-biography of Early Life	Gospel of Grace to the Gentiles	Law vs. Grace	Freedom in Christ	Walk Free in the Spirit	Exhortations
Paragraph Titles	:1–5 Greeting :6–10 One true gospel to preach :11–17 Paul's commission to preach :18–24 Paul's reputation in Jerusalem	:1–10 Approval of apostles :11–12 Paul confronts Peter	:1–14 Laws not the way :15–22 Jesus and the law :23–29 Oneness in Christ	:1–7 Rights of sonship in Christ :8–11 Freemen returning to slavery :12–20 Paul's disappointment :21–31 Illustration of Isaac & Ishmael	:1 Stay free :2–12 Legalism excluded :13–15 Love is the outcome of freedom :16–24 Walk in the Spirit :25–26 Humility in the Spirit	:1–5 Bear one another's burdens :6–10 Reaping in the Spirit :11–16 Boast only in the cross :17–18 Summary testimony and closing
Key Verse:	12	2	13	31	22	10
Key Word:	Revelation	Gentiles	Law	Free	Spirit	Reap

*Michael Z.

Step One

How to "See It"

A Guide to Observation

Chapter 3: Ask the Right Questions
Learning What to Look For

Early in my ministry with Campus Crusade for Christ, I was assigned to Argentina. Imagine my culture shock when I discovered that their favorite sport is not American football or basketball but soccer. The first time I watched a soccer game, I was utterly confused. I had no idea what was going on. I was totally ignorant of the rules, the strategy, or even what was supposed to happen on the field. But after seeing several soccer matches and listening to explanations, I learned the rules and the subtleties of player moves and strategy. I began to anticipate plays, and even shouted advice to the players—and the referees. I now knew what to look for and that knowledge increased my appreciation and enjoyment of the game tremendously.

The same is true in Bible study. If you don't learn some of the "ins and outs" of what the book is about, you will not know what to look for. You will find the Bible confusing and uninteresting. It will be merely something you read because you know you should or as a nice source of occasional inspiration. But when you learn to see beneath the surface of the words of the Bible, the many facets of God's revelation will begin to shimmer for you. It is crucial, therefore, to develop an approach to observation that will enable you, with the help of the Holy Spirit, to understand what God wants to show you in the Bible.

Learning to observe helps you see what is really there. The FBI uses training films to teach agents the art of observation. One of these films is three minutes long and shows a train robbery. Accompanying the film is a list of over one hundred questions testing what agents observe on seeing the film for the first time.

The list includes such questions as, "Was the man left-handed?" "What was in his back pocket?" "Did the woman wear a watch?" And so on.

I know of a seminary professor who shows this film in his Bible study methods class. The average score is thirty-five correct answers to the more than one hundred questions. But one year an ex-FBI agent took the professor's course. He had never seen that particular training film, yet he answered every question correctly. What was the key? He knew what to look for.

Not knowing what to look for is only one deterrent to learning to "see it." Another is not knowing *how* to look. It's like witnessing. People who don't know how to witness usually do not witness. People who don't know how to look into the Bible usually quit looking into the Bible. They may read it, but they fail to see the meaning of what they read. Many people miss the meaning of great art because they don't know how to look at a painting. You've seen it happen in museums: One group of visitors will pass a painting and shake their heads and laugh or make a glib wisecrack about it. The next group will stop and gaze at the same painting in breathless awe, excitedly discussing with each other the meaning and impact of the piece. Why such different responses? The second group knows how to see a painting. They understand such things as movement, form, gesture, harmony, and composition—all the elements that make a painting communicate. That is why you sometimes hear people say that we don't judge paintings; paintings judge us. The same can be said of those who claim they can't get anything out of the Bible. Their failure says more about them than about the book.

A third deterrent to effective Bible study is simply failure to look. As Chesterton said, "Christianity has not been tried and found wanting; it has been found hard and not tried." I'm afraid that describes the approach of many to Bible study. Once they realize it's not just going to pop off the page, they close the book and abandon the effort. They fail to look, therefore they do not see. As I said earlier, there's no easy method, no special shortcut. Bible study takes effort. But the rewards are tremendously satisfying. Knowledge of God and his Word will lead to a changed life.

The Six Basic Questions

In Bible study we learn how to look and what to look for by asking those six key questions we all learned in the third grade:

For ease in studying, a printable version of these questions is available (information regarding how to obtain this is in Appendix A, page 159). Never mind that this seems like a grade school approach. Journalists ask these questions with every story they write because these six questions are effective probing tools. They force one to penetrate the surface and dig out all the pertinent information available. I have found them equally effective in delving into the meaning of Scripture; they are my tools for probing beneath the surface of the passage. These questions help me to see what is really there.

For that reason I sometimes call these six basic questions "surfacers" because they bring information to the surface that may not be immediately obvious. Think of these questions as spades to be used in digging for buried treasure. They probe deeply into a passage and bring to the surface hidden thoughts and meanings. These questions help us to learn how to look. When you study a given passage, the "Who?" spade brings to the surface information about the personalities it mentions. The "Where?" spade brings up the places. You get the idea.

Now let's consider how these basic questions work. For the "Who?" question, let's look at John 1:21 where the question is actually asked for us in the passage itself. After John the Baptist denies that he is the Messiah, the Jewish leaders ask, "Well then, who are you?" That's the question you need to answer for your study. Just who is John the Baptist? You can find answers in other passages, including John's own answer in the next three verses.

The second question is "What?" What is the passage saying? What is happening? If people are mentioned in the passage, what did they do? What caused their actions? The list of "What?" questions can become quite long.

Next you ask "When?" When did the event in the passage occur? Or, if the passage is prophetic, when will it occur? Or even, when can it occur? The "When?" question brings the dimension of time into play. It locates the event historically in the past or prophetically in the future. The "When?" question can help you to relate one passage with another when their times coincide, or when a prophetic passage in the Old Testament matches up with its fulfillment in the New Testament.

The fourth question is "Where?" Where did the event described happen? Where is the character involved going? Where will the prophetic fulfillment take place?

The fifth question, "Why?" helps you delve into motivations and reasons. Why did he say that? Why did he go there? Why did he do that?

Finally we ask "How?" How did the event of the passage happen? How could it happen? How will it happen? The question "How?" involves process. How was the wall of Jerusalem built in Nehemiah's day? How was Jesus crucified? How did Jesus heal the blind man in John 9? Or the "How?" question can uncover more than just factual information. You can use it to explore the emotion of the passage. How do circumstances affect the attitude of Bible characters? If you were the blind man in John 9, how would you feel if Christ healed you?

Feel free to use your own methods and procedures in asking these six basic questions. Some students ask "Who?" of all the verses in a chapter before they ask the next questions. Others prefer to ask all six basic questions of each verse as they go. It's your call.

The Observation Chart

As you ask these six basic questions, how do you capture the answers? You make an Observation Chart. A sample of this chart is on page 47 at the end of this chapter, so let's look at each column of the chart and work through the process of filling it in. (Again, for a printable version of this chart see Appendix A, page 159.)

Column 1: Scripture

The first column is where you place your Scripture. You can enter your Scripture in either of two ways: You can simply enter the reference ("John 1:10," for example) or you can enter the entire text of the verse, but I personally prefer to have the entire verse right there in front of me. If you are working on a computer, I suggest entering the entire verse; it's easy to copy it from computer Bible software or an online resource and just paste it into your column.

Column 2: Observations

The center column is the heart of the chart. It's where you enter your observations after you study your passage. Your entries may include any spontaneous observations that come to you as you read, but most of them will be information you uncover as you ask the six basic questions. The "Observations" column is where you place the answers to these questions. This column displays the end result of your observation study.

Column 3: Questions

If the "Observations" column is the end result of your study, the "Questions" column is the process. The "Scripture" column contains the raw material, the "Observations" column is the warehouse, and the "Questions" column is the factory where information is processed. Most of the work, naturally, is done in the factory. Therefore we will spend quite a bit of time in the "Questions" column.

I will now show you how to use the questions as tools to dig out what you need to see and how to use the chart to facilitate the process and record the results. We will use John 3:1–2a as our Scripture passage to learn on. "There was a man named Nicodemus, a Jewish religious leader who was a Pharisee. After dark one evening, he came to speak with Jesus." There's the passage; now let's start asking our questions.

Question 1: Who? The first question we want to answer is "Who?" So enter the word "who" in the "Observations" column—this is where the answers to your questions will go. I usually box the word, write it in bold, or underscore it so it jumps right out

Ask the Right Questions

at me. It's your heading above the space where you will record the answer to the question "Who?" after you determine what that answer is.

Next you will go to the "Questions" column and enter all the questions this passage raises in your mind. Do this now before you read on, then come back and we will compare notes.

OK, after you've entered your "Who?" questions, compare them with mine: "Who was Nicodemus? Who were the Pharisees? Who were the Jewish religious leaders? These seem to me the natural questions this passage would raise.

Now take the first question, "Who was Nicodemus?" and spend another few minutes to see how many observations you can make from it. Then come back and we'll compare again...

Are you back? Okay, here's what the passage showed me in answer to the question, "Who was Nicodemus?" He was a *man*; he was a *Pharisee*; his name was *Nicodemus*; he was a *ruler*; he was a *Jew*. All this we glean from verse 1 (verse 10 tells us he was also a teacher). In a sense you "know" all these things simply by reading the sentence, but you probably never focused on these details. It took the question "Who?" to make you stop and study and see more deeply instead of merely skimming and forgetting. Enter these answers in the "Observations" column under your word, "Who?"

These observations that sprang from the "Who?" question spawn all kinds of additional questions: What was a Pharisee? How did a man become a Pharisee? What did a Pharisee do? What was the relationship of a Pharisee to a ruler? How did one qualify to become a Pharisee? What education was necessary? What is a Jew? What is a ruler? Obviously most of these are not "Who?" questions, but you need to write all of them down in your "Questions" column as you think of them. You will find them useful at our next step of study, which is interpretation. You may choose to answer only those most pertinent to your study, but write down all questions you think of so you won't forget them. Decide later which are important. Remember, these charts are not your final study product; they are the process. They are simply for information capture.

Question 2: When? Look again at our example passage, John 3:1–2: "Nicodemus was a Pharisee and a member of the Jewish council. He came to Jesus one night and said to him, 'Rabbi, we know that God has sent you as a teacher. No one can perform the miracles you perform unless God is with him'" (GWT). The passage answers the "When?" question in the second verse: Nicodemus came to Jesus "after dark." Before we explore this, I want to mention a problem you will sometimes encounter. It often happens that you will find nothing to answer any one of your six interpretive questions in a given passage. In fact, if you are reading John 3:1–2 from some other translation rather than the GOD'S WORD® Translation, the question "When?" may not be answered in the second verse. When a verse has nothing to answer one of your six questions, you don't put the question aside and go to the next question; instead, you move on to the next verse to see if it provides an answer.

In your "Observations" column under "When?" you write "after dark," or "at night." This answer to our "When?" question is quite intriguing and hints at mystery. It propels us immediately to the next question, "Why?"

Question 3: Why? Why did Nicodemus come to Jesus after dark? Use your imagination. Put yourself in Nicodemus's situation and ask why you might have come to Jesus after dark instead of in broad daylight. Write down any reason that comes to mind. Don't be concerned with whether you are correct; you will determine which answers fit the truth later as we go through the steps of interpretation. At this point, the whole idea of the exercise is to immerse yourself in the passage. I repeat that these charts are not the final product but merely the working process. So don't hesitate to record your speculations.

Your thinking might go something like this: Suppose you are a Jew, a Pharisee, a ruler, and a teacher—that is, a respected member of the cream of the Jewish community. Why would you choose to see Jesus at night? Let's list the possible reasons under the steps of observation.

The first possibility is that Nicodemus didn't want anyone to see him. Why wouldn't he want anyone to see him? Could it be fear of the Pharisees, the Jews, the teachers, or the rulers? Or could it be pride? If he was a great teacher in the Jewish religious establishment and Jesus had gained a rivaling reputation as a great teacher, is it possible that Nicodemus would feel belittled in the eyes of his peers if any of them saw him visiting this unauthorized upstart?

Why else might Nicodemus choose to see Jesus after dark? Perhaps the reason is not so mysterious after all. He may simply have been too busy to get away in the daytime. As a teacher and a leader, maybe his day was filled with meetings, appointments, and classes. We can certainly identify with that. Or maybe he just wanted to talk with Jesus alone to discuss things not meant for the ears of others. The daytime crowds around Jesus would have made private conversations impossible. (It's ironic to consider that if this was his reasoning, his plan certainly backfired. The entire world has read the content of that private conversation for two thousand years.)

Let's pause here and summarize our speculative answers in outline form:

> **Why did Nicodemus come to see Jesus after dark?**
>
> I. So no one else would see him
>   A. Because of fear
>   1. of Pharisees
>   2. of rulers
>   3. of Jews
>   4. of teachers
>   B. Because of pride
>   1. Protect teaching reputation
>   2. Jesus unauthorized upstart
> II. Too busy in daytime
> III. Wanted to talk alone

Simply by asking the first three questions we begin to get insights into the passage. In fact, by exploring possibilities and motivations, we are getting inside the passage and feeling its impact. Now that you see how the process works, we will skim a little faster through the next three questions. I will give you a little guidance in asking the questions, and you can think of answers on your own using the methods we've already discussed.

Question 4: What? Do you see anything in our sample passage of which you can ask, "What?" I see several: What was a Pharisee? What did a Pharisee do? What was the relationship of a Pharisee to a ruler? What education was necessary? What was a teacher in first-century Judea? What is a Jew? What is a ruler? Write down all these questions in your "Questions" column. Unlike the speculative answers you must give when asking questions about a man's motives (as when asking why Nicodemus came to Jesus by night), these questions have definite answers. And some of the answers will not be found by simple observation because the Bible does not explain them. That means the answers will involve interpretation, which we will explore in our next study step. To find them will require a little research. Therefore, we will not address these questions in our observation step, but you need to record them in your "Questions" column to be addressed when we explore interpretation.

Question 5: How? Let's look at our Scripture passage again to see if it answers any "How?" questions. "There was a man named Nicodemus, a Jewish religious leader who was a Pharisee. After dark one evening, he came to speak with Jesus." A few questions come to mind immediately. How did a man become a Pharisee? How did one qualify? How did Nicodemus know of Jesus? How did he know where to find him? Some of these questions are speculative and some require research to provide definitive answers. Write them down to be addressed in the interpretation step.

Question 6: Where? Here's a case in which our passage does not answer the "Where?" question. As I said above, more often than not you will find that all questions do not apply to each passage. But you need to ask the question anyway. It is designed to elicit information and be sure that you don't overlook anything the passage offers. So instead of laying the question aside, you should move on to the next verses until you either find one that addresses the question or until you complete the thought of the passage and find that no answer is forthcoming.

You can see by doing this exercise how it's possible to spend hours delving into a single verse. You may find this impossible or discouraging. As much as you would like to spend all of your time every evening doing nothing more than Bible study, your time may be limited. One good thing about the method I'm presenting here is that you can spend as much or as little time as you have on it. If all you have is fifteen minutes every evening, do what you can in fifteen minutes. Over the days, it adds up. And at the end of that time you will know more than if you did not do the study. The key is to spend whatever time you do have, whether it's fifteen minutes, a half hour, or forty-five minutes. Sometimes you may find time available outside your regular study hours. Think how many of these questions you might answer on a fifty-minute plane trip or during the time you spend in the airport waiting for the boarding call.

Assignment

Using chapter 1 of the book of John, complete an Observation Chart.

Ask the Right Questions

Observation Chart		
Scripture	Observations	Questions

Chapter 4: Dig Deeper
Probing Beneath the Surface

The boy came to his father and asked, "Dad, what's a black hole?"

"I really don't know, son," the father answered.

Several minutes later the boy appeared again and asked, "Dad, what is electricity?"

The father thought for a moment, then replied, "I really can't say, son."

After a while the boy came in a third time and asked, "Dad, what is gravity?"

"I just don't know, son," responded the father again.

The boy then said, "Dad, do you get tired of me asking all these questions?"

"Oh no, of course not, son," replied the father. "How will you ever learn if you don't ask questions?"

Well, I hope you're not tired of asking questions. In Bible study, questions are truly the way to learn. In considering the six basic questions of the previous chapter we've only scratched the surface. Now we will learn how to ask the twelve relationship questions. The purpose of relationship questions is to add another dimension to your knowledge by helping you examine how terms, people, places, or ideas in one passage of Scripture interconnect with those of other passages. If this makes little sense to you now, don't be concerned. In this chapter I will explain and demonstrate how it works. You will place the observations that result from these questions in the center column of your Observation Chart.

Here are the twelve relationship questions:

> 1. What things are alike or similar?
> 2. What things are different?
> 3. What things are repeated?
> 4. What evidences of cause and effect do you see?
> 5. What movement from the general to the specific do you see?
> 6. What progressions are evident?
> 7. What questions or answers are given?
> 8. What problem and solution are presented?
> 9. In what way might the length of the passage be significant?
> 10. What relationship words are used?
> 11. What commands do you see?
> 12. What promises do you see?

After spending a chapter learning to process six questions, the prospect of facing twelve more may overwhelm you. It shouldn't. In a passage such as John 3:1–10, you can go through our first six questions and these twelve questions in as little as thirty minutes. Of course, you can spend more time if you have it available. The answers to these questions will not come automatically. You must keep your mind alert and open to comparisons or you will not find them. But these questions will help you work through the process.

To make the application of these questions a little easier for you, they are listed on a single sheet as a reproducible bonus resource (see Appendix A, page 159).

Now let's go over these questions one by one to see how you can use them as digging tools to uncover knowledge of the Scripture. In the next chapter we will hone in on one question to demonstrate in depth how you can use it to probe as deeply as you want into a given passage.

1. What things are alike or similar?

This question is designed to help you look for comparisons as you read a passage. Remember, the reason people do not see things in Scripture is that they don't know what to look for. These questions isolate things you should look for. If you look specifically for things that are alike or similar, you are more apt to see them.

Let's say you have already done your study of John 3 and you are now working on John 4. As you read of Jesus' encounter with the Samaritan woman, you begin looking for comparisons. What things are alike or similar to other passages you have already studied in John 3? In both chapters Christ had opportunities to witness—first to Nicodemus and then to the Samaritan woman. Ask the first relationship question: what are the similarities between these two encounters? You might come up with the following answers:

- Both encounters were one-on-one.
- Both involved people interested in religion.
- In both cases Christ guided the conversation toward spiritual things.
- In both cases Christ honed in on key issues.
- Christ refused to get sidetracked into secondary controversies.

These similarities broaden your understanding of Christ by showing his single-mindedness in giving the people he encountered exactly what they needed to know to come to him. It also shows that regardless of differences in station or background, the essential needs of all people are the same—they all need Christ.

You may enter these and any other observations spurred by the question in the center column of your Observation Chart.

2. What things are different?

With this question, you do the opposite of what the first question asks. You look not for similarities but for contrasts. When we apply this question to John 3 and 4, we notice several significant differences between Nicodemus and the Samaritan woman, as the following chart shows.

Differences Between Nicodemus and the Samaritan Woman	
John 3 (Nicodemus)	John 4 (Samaritan woman)
A man	A woman
A Jew	A Samaritan
Socially prominent	Social outcast
Comes by night	Comes in daytime
Still questioning	Comes to faith
Judaism	Samaritan religion
Religious leader	Religious pagan
Ashamed	Bold

Do the number of contrasts surprise you? Can you see how these contrasts make these two passages parallel to each other? The contrasts help us to understand why John has the event in chapter 4 follow that of chapter 3. Two people encounter Christ: one was religious, high on the social scale, and well respected; the other was an adulterous social outcast. Yet Christ ignores all differences and treats both equally, showing great interest in both and leading them to a greater understanding of the truth.

3. What things are repeated?

Over and over in the book of John, Jesus used the phrase, "I assure you..." or "I tell you the truth" ("Verily, verily, I say unto thee..." in some translations). This repetition indicates that Jesus was interested in overcoming doubt with truth. He repeatedly affirmed the absolute truth of what he said. This is not *a* truth, but *the* truth. Often words, phrases, or ideas are repeated to aid learning or to add emphasis. Watch for such repetitions and, when you find them, ask why they are repeated. The reason may help you uncover an insight that would otherwise have remained hidden.

4. What evidences of cause and effect do you see?

Cause and effect means that one thing leads to another. Sometimes passages containing cause and effect won't jump out at you, but certain words will give you a clue: words that link cause to effect are *because, for, therefore,* or *since*. When *because* is used, the effect usually comes before the cause, as in John 10:17: "The Father loves me because I sacrifice my life so I may take it back again." The effect is the love of the Father for Jesus. The cause is that Jesus loves so much that he sacrifices his life. What we learn is that Christ's sacrificial love for us endears him to the Father. Cause and effect shows relationships that enhance our understanding of Scripture.

5. What movement from the general to the specific do you see?

This kind of movement happens often in Scripture. In John 1:10, we read this general statement about Christ: "He came into the very world he created, but the world didn't recognize him." Then in verse 11 we have the specific statement, "He came to his own people, and even they rejected him." Notice how the first general statement sets up the second specific one. The general principle is that the whole world didn't recognize Christ; his rejection by his own people is the specific instance of the principle. What does this mean to us? First, Israel is presented as a microcosm of an attitude toward Christ that always exists wherever his name is known. Second, we learn from later events that eventually the world outside Judea accepted Christ while the Jewish nation remained entrenched in its unbelief. The very people specifically charged with the honor and responsibility of bringing the Savior to the world failed to partake of that salvation.

6. What progressions are evident?

Look for an idea or an event building, developing, or unfolding. Often the progression will climax with a specific act or idea. For example, the entire book of John shows such a progression. Jesus' public ministry began slowly and moved with increasing visibility and conflict until it climaxed in his triumphal entry into Jerusalem, which initiated the passion week, culminating in the crucifixion.

We find an example of progression in a specific passage in John 4, a passage we've already mined for other jewels. First Jesus goes through Samaria. He stops in Sychar, at the ancient well of Jacob. He meets a woman drawing water. He enters a conversation with her. It leads to her confronting her sin, and then to her conversion. She tells her friends, who also come out to hear Jesus, and soon the entire village is converted. That's progression!

7. What questions or answers are given?

Questions and answers often carry arguments that culminate in teaching important biblical principles. Questions force one to think, examine the issues, and stay on target. When a teacher attempts to drive home a point, he or she will often use questions to elicit the answer desired. Questions can also be used simply to search for answers we don't know. In John 3:4, Nicodemus asks Jesus, "How can an old man go back into his mother's womb and be born again?" The question gives Jesus the opportunity to explain the whole Christian concept of new birth and kingdom life—a concept as important for us today as it was for Nicodemus.

8. What problem and solution are presented?

Problems and their solutions often capture important insights into the meaning of Scripture. We find an example of a problem in John 2:1–3. At a wedding feast in Cana, the host has run out of wine, a terrible social *faux pas* in first-century Judean culture. In verse 3 Jesus' mother Mary presents the problem to him, and then in verses 6–10 we have the solution when Jesus turns water into wine, saving the day for the wedding hosts. In verse 11 we are given the reason for this solution: "This miraculous sign at Cana in Galilee was the first time Jesus revealed his glory. And his disciples believed in him." The problem led to the solution, and the solution provided the introduction of Christ's power, bringing many people to belief.

9. Is the length of the passage significant?

When the tsunami disaster of 2005 killed over 150,000 people in the countries around the Indian Ocean, the story filled the front pages of the national newspapers for days. On the other hand, when the local bank president spoke at the community Rotary Club, the city paper allotted only a short paragraph to the speech. The importance of the story determines the space allotment. The same principle applies to Scripture. The Bible writers filled the most space with the most important principles and incidents, allotting only a few verses or less to those less important. John 1:29–12:50 covers incidents in the three-year ministry of Jesus. Then in chapter 13, John shifts down and spends five chapters on Jesus and the Last Supper with his disciples, two chapters on his arrest, trial, and death, and two chapters on his resurrection and post-resurrection appearances.

Does John spending twelve chapters on three years and five chapters on one night indicate any kind of emphasis on Jesus' final words to his disciples? This is the kind of thing you can determine from paying attention to the space allotment an author gives to a given subject. If he slows down and treats a short period of time in great detail, we students will be wise to do the same thing. Look hard for the reasons for the emphasis and spend more time digging into those passages for their meaning. The author's emphasis shows where he wants you to focus.

10. What relationship words are used?

By relationship words I mean connecting words such as *but*, *since*, *and*, *if*, *therefore*, and other conjunctions. We addressed some of these words when we discussed cause and effect, but here we note that these and other connectors also show relationships between one event and another or one idea and another. For example, in John 8:12 Jesus says, "I am the light of the world. If you follow me, you won't have to walk in darkness." In this passage *if* connects two thoughts and shows the relationship between them. One thought is *following Jesus*. The other is *you won't have to walk in darkness*. You must do the first to bring about the second. The connecting *if* shows a relationship of dependence of the second idea to the first.

Watch for *conditional connectives* such as "if—then." "If—then" statements set down specific conditions for fulfillment. *If* you do certain things, *then* God will do certain things. Some of the newer translations do not use this construction, but omit the word, "then." In such cases "then" is often implied. For example, look at 1 John 1:9 in the NLT: "But if we confess our sins to him, [then] he is faithful and just to forgive us our sins and to cleanse us from all wickedness." The connectors are critical to the meaning of the passage because they show the conditional nature of the promise: *If* we confess our sins, *then* he will forgive us. The conditional connectives show that the promise is not without qualification.

Also watch for *connectives of purpose* such as "in order that" or "because of." Connectives of purpose give the reason or the *purpose* of a given action. Again, varying construction in different translations causes these phrases to appear in some Bibles but not in others. We have a connective of purpose in Philippians 3:12 (NASB): "Not that I have already obtained it, or have already become perfect, but I press on in order that I may lay hold of that for which also I was laid hold of by Christ Jesus." Why does Paul press on? The *in order that* phrase tells us: so that he can gain the prize Christ called him to.

The chart on page 59 at the end of this chapter provides you with a list of various connectors and their significance. I suggest that you obtain a copy of this page and use it as a study tool (see Appendix A on page 159 for Bonus Resources).

11. What commands do you see?

Always be alert for commands in the Bible. These are important for obvious reasons: They may apply to us today.

12. What promises do you see?

Be alert for any of God's promises and consider any conditions that may be attached to them. While commands are important for practical reasons, promises are important because they are inspirational and give us hope.

Assignment

Make observations from John 2 on your chart using the twelve relationship questions discussed in this chapter.

Dig Deeper

Significant Words to Look For in Bible Passages

1. Logical connectors:

    a. Contrast
    - but (Ephesians 2:4)
    - even though (Romans 1:21)
    - much more (Romans 5:15)
    - nevertheless (Romans 5:33)
    - yet (Romans 5:8)
    - although
    - then
    - otherwise (Romans 11:6)

    b. Comparison
    - too (Ephesians 2:3)
    - also (Ephesians 1:11)
    - as (Ephesians 5:22)
    - just as (Ephesians 4:32)
    - so also (Ephesians 5:28)
    - likewise (1 Peter 3:7)
    - and
    - like

    c. Correlatives
    - as... so also (Ephesians 5:24)
    - for... as (Ephesians 5:23)
    - so... as (Ephesians 5:28)

    d. Reason
    - because (Ephesians 2:4)
    - for this reason... (Ephesians 3:15)
    - for this purpose (Ephesians 6:22)
    - for (Ephesians 2:8)
    - since (Colossians 1:4)

    e. Result
    - so then (Ephesians 2:19)
    - therefore (Ephesians 2:11)
    - as a result (Ephesians 4:14)
    - thus
    - then

    f. Purpose/Result
    - that (Ephesians 1:4)
    - so that (Ephesians 1:18)
    - in order that (Ephesians 4:28)

    g. Condition
    - if (Ephesians 3:2)

2. Temporal or time connectors:
    - now (Ephesians 2:2)
    - until (Ephesians 4:13)
    - when (Ephesians 1:20)
    - before (Ephesians 1:4)
    - after (Ephesians 1:13)
    - while (Ephesians 1:16)
    - since (Colossians 3:1)

3. Geographical connectors:
    - where (Colossians 3:1)

Chapter 5: See How It Works
Stepping Through the Process

To demonstrate how the twelve relationship questions work, let's do a more thorough exercise based on a passage we've already considered. We will look again at John 4, where Jesus met the Samaritan woman at the well in Sychar. Using passages from this chapter we will give examples of how the process of using basic questions and relationship questions will dig out the kind of information you need for good Bible study.

The little drama played out in this chapter has only two main characters, Jesus and the Samaritan woman. We already know who Jesus is, and now we want to know more about the woman. As we read about her, let's start the discovery process by asking the first basic question, "Who?" Who was this woman? Can we determine much about her identity and character from information in this chapter? The answer is yes; the passage reveals quite a bit about her when you start asking who she was. Here is a list of my answers:

1. She was a Samaritan (v. 9).
2. She was sensitive to the Jew-Samaritan racial issue (v. 9).
3. She was a nationalist—proud of her heritage (v. 12).
4. She did not like to draw water (v. 15).
5. She was a prostitute or an adulteress (v. 18).
6. She was a religious formalist—she thought there was only one way to worship (v. 20).
7. She was hungry to know the Messiah (vv. 25, 28–29).

As a result of our interpretive "Who?" question, we have learned quite a bit about who this Samaritan woman is. So let's sample the next step of the process by asking the first two relationship questions of our main characters. The first question is, "What things are alike and similar?" In these verses we find that both Jesus and the Samaritan woman:

1. were physically thirsty (v. 7).
2. had a common heritage in Jacob (v. 12).
3. had an interest in spiritual things (v. 19–28).
4. had an obvious interest in speaking with each other.

Enter what you've gleaned from this question on your chart in the "Observations" column.

When you get into the process, often your observations will reach past the simple, obvious statement of the text and leap into broader principles. For example, you may see Jesus' commonality with people in his conversation with the Samaritan woman. He loved each one he encountered, even those low on the social scale like this woman. You may observe that his humanity gave him the same physical needs as the rest of us. He was tired and thirsty as he sat at the well. You may see how the woman was obviously drawn to Jesus who, as she quickly perceived, could satisfy her spiritual hunger. Enter these larger observations along with the basic ones on your Observation Chart.

Now let's move to the second relationship question, "What things are different?" We did a similar exercise in the previous chapter where we contrasted Nicodemus with the Samaritan woman, showing the differences between the person Jesus encountered in John 3 and the one he encountered in John 4. This time we will show the differences, or contrasts, between Jesus and the Samaritan woman.

After asking the question and observing the differences, write them down on your Observation Chart.

Differences	
Woman	Jesus
Adulteress	Son of God, Rabbi
Woman	Man
Samaritan	Jew
Samaritan religion	Judaism
From Samaria	From Judea

I'm going to pause here for a moment and mention a few things we will explore more thoroughly in the next couple of chapters. In those chapters I will explain the next step after observation, which is interpretation. In the interpretation step you will ask of these differences between Jesus and the Samaritan woman, "What do they mean? How do they affect relationship and communication? Do they create barriers, or are they insignificant?" To uncover these answers, you will want to go back to the question, "What?" Look at each difference and ask, "What barrier would this difference create between Jesus and the Samaritan woman?"

At this point you will find that simple observation of the text will not give you all the answers you need. External research will be necessary in answering these questions. The answers you glean from these resources will not be merely observation, but interpretation, for they will go beyond what you see in the text to an exploration of the meaning of the text. I will explain the interpretation step fully in the next chapters, but here I suggest that you do not observe these Bible study steps rigidly. Move in and out of observation and interpretation as you explore. For now, while you're exploring the contrasts between Jesus and the woman, you need to do one of two things: Either you need to move temporarily into the interpretation step and answer your interpretation questions while the subject is on your mind, or you need to record your interpretation questions as they occur to you so you can answer them when you do move into the interpretation step.

It is obvious from the text that Jesus was highly effective in breaking through the barriers that separated him from the Samaritan woman. Therefore the "How?" question pops up. How did he do it?

First, he ignored any tradition that stood in his way, no matter how long-standing. We read in John 4:3–4, "So he left Judea and returned to Galilee. He had to go through Samaria on the way." Judea and Galilee were both Jewish provinces under the control of the Roman empire. Samaria lay between them. The Jews despised the Samaritans so much that when they needed to travel from Judea to Galilee, they would not journey through Samaria but would go all the way around it to keep from touching Samaritan soil. But, as verses 3 and 4 tell us, Jesus went through Samaria. He ignored the spiteful, degrading tradition and walked boldly down Samaritan roads. He also ignored the traditions of not talking with a sinner, a woman, and a Samaritan.

Second, Jesus used a little psychology to weaken any barrier that might have been erected in the woman's mind. No doubt having been shunned by Jews all her life, and probably even shunned by her own people because of her blatant sins, she likely would never have entered a conversation with this Jew sitting at the well. So look at what Jesus did to break through this barrier: He asked for a favor. "Please give me a drink," he said. One way to get a person to like you is to ask for a favor. It makes the person feel that you are indebted to him in some small way, and it gives the person confidence because he is not placed in an inferior position. Basically, people like to help others. It makes them feel good.

In recording your observations on how Jesus broke through the barriers, you might write on your chart, "He ignored traditions (went through Samaria)," and "He asked for a favor (a drink of water)."

In this chapter we are not trying to complete a chart for you, but merely give you a few examples of how to elicit information from the text by using the questions. So let's skip over questions 3–5 and address relationship question 6: "What progressions are evident?" Remember that a progression is an idea or an event building, developing, or unfolding, often climaxing with a specific act or idea.

Do we have any indication of progression in John 4? Indeed we do. Jesus' witness to the Samaritan woman gives us a classic example showing how a simple, seemingly chance meeting resulted in the salvation of many villagers. As I asked the question about progression, I found four instances in the conversation with the woman in which Jesus led her up to a higher level of thought. Let's identify them.

First, Jesus offered the Samaritan woman something desirable (vv. 10, 13–14). What was one thing this woman longed for? She would have loved to have a source of water in her house to eliminate the daily walk to the well in the hot sun where she no doubt endured the scorn of the other women. Jesus offered her water so rich that she would never thirst again. Naturally, she was intrigued. "'Please, sir,' the woman said, 'give me this water! Then I'll never be thirsty again, and I won't have to come here to get water'" (v. 15). She wanted that water, but she obviously didn't understand the spiritual nature of the offer.

Second, Jesus told the woman why she could not have the water he offered. Her sin stood in the way. He had to expose her sin so she could remove it. Notice how subtly he did it. Instead of thundering, "It's because of your horrible sin!" he perceptively put her on the spot by saying, "Go and get your husband" (v. 16). The woman responded immediately: "I don't have a husband" (v. 17). "You're right!" Jesus emphatically agreed. "You don't have a husband—for you have had five husbands, and you aren't even married to the man you're living with now." He raised the level of the conversation. It progressed from a seemingly simple request to an exposure of the woman's deep problem that kept her from finding the peace she sought.

The woman was shocked that Jesus could know all this. She realized she was in the presence of a prophet, obviously a religious man. She tried to escape the personal probe into her life by changing the subject to one that would surely divert this man of God—religion. "Sir," the woman said, "you must be a prophet. So tell me, why is it that you Jews insist that Jerusalem is the only place of worship, while we Samaritans claim it is here at Mount Gerizim, where our ancestors worshiped?" (vv. 19–20).

The woman's attempt at diversion enabled Jesus to move the conversation to the third level of progression. We see that he refused to be drawn into an argument, and instead introduced the concept that devotion to God is not dependent on any certain place, but on knowing the one you worship. His answer told her not to get bogged down in peripherals such as place; true worship is that which is done in spirit and in truth (vv. 21–24). It's not about going to this mountain or that city; it's about the reality of God and getting one's heart right with him. He moved her from exposure of sin to the need to know God. The conversation progressed up another notch.

Then the woman herself set up the fourth progression with her next response. Apparently she was not quite buying into Jesus' answer. Though she was drawn to what he said, she would not take his word that her long-standing tradition of mountain worship could be wrong and that worship is a matter of spirit and truth. But, rather than argue the point, she attempted escape by appealing to an authority that was not yet available to settle the question, thus still evading the implications of where Jesus was leading her. She said, "I know the Messiah is coming—the one who is called Christ. When he comes, he will explain everything to us."

That response gave Jesus the opportunity he needed to deliver the clincher: "I Am the Messiah!" All the authority she needed for truth was standing right there in front of her eyes. He was the water she thirsted for, the truth she sought, the answer to her needs. In this final step he challenged her faith. Will she believe or not? We find later that she does believe (vv. 39–42). Through four progressive steps, Jesus led her to him.

You might enter on your chart these observations from your progression question:

1. Jesus offers her something desirable.
2. He tells her why she cannot have it.
3. He tells her what God requires.
4. He challenges her to believe.

The more you learn to look, the more you find. Do you also see a parallel progression in the woman's attitude toward Christ as they converse? In verse 9 she called him a Jew, a slanderous term to a Samaritan. In verse 11, she addressed him as "sir"—a polite term showing respect. In verse 19, she called him a prophet, and then in verse 29 she told people he was the Messiah.

We can also see a progression in the evangelistic results of her encounter with Jesus:

1. She encountered the Christ (v. 26).
2. She told others, apparently in a matter of minutes (v. 29).
3. On her testimony, others believed in Christ (v. 39).
4. Others encountered Christ and believed (v. 41).

Now let's apply another relationship question to the text. Question 4 asks, "What evidences of cause and effect do you see?" Look at verse 28: "The woman left her water jar beside the well and ran back to the village." The fact that she left her water jar—a valuable commodity in that time—shows her excitement and haste. She couldn't wait to spread the news about Jesus. This sudden action of hers is an effect. What was the cause? We find it in verse 26, when Jesus said to her, "I Am the Messiah." That stunning revelation caused her to leave her water jar and run into town to tell others.

But interestingly, her action was not only an effect but also a cause in itself that led to another effect. We see this effect in verses 39–42 where we read that, as a result of her testimony, many of the villagers came out to hear Jesus and believed in him. Thus, by asking the cause and effect question, we find that not only was the woman converted, her conversion had a tremendous impact on the entire town. It led to a revival.

Now we will ask relationship question 5: "What movement from the general to the specific do you see?" Look at the opening of the conversation between Jesus and the woman. They begin talking about water. At first the topic is water in general—the clear, liquid, drinkable H_2O stuff. But Jesus quickly narrowed the meaning, using water as a metaphor with a spiritual connotation. With the spiritual established as his subject, he spoke of the Father (v. 23), and from the Father he moved the subject to himself, the Messiah (v. 26). He moved the conversation from something very general (water) to something quite specific—himself.

Next we will go to relationship question 7: "What questions or answers are given?" We find Jesus asking a question in verse 35: "You know the saying, 'Four months between planting and harvest.' But I say, wake up and look around. The fields are already ripe for harvest." A question like this spurs you to ask a couple of basic questions: *Who* was Jesus talking to? *What* did he mean by it? When we look back to verse 31, we find the answer to the "Who?" question: he was talking to his disciples. When we read forward through verse 38, we find the answer to the "what" question. Jesus himself explained it. He was using crop harvest as a metaphor for winning souls. He explained to these disciples that bringing people to belief has no season because the need exists all the time. People's hearts are being prepared continually, and his disciples were being prepared to reap these souls that God was ripening for harvest.

We see another question in verse 32 that gives us a clue to what Jesus was doing here. Just as he finished his conversation with the Samaritan woman, the disciples returned with lunch and urged him to eat. He told them, "I have a kind of food you know nothing about." Naturally they assumed he was speaking of physical meat and bread and they wondered where he got it, so they asked each other, "Did someone bring him food while we were gone?"

At that moment the disciples were mainly concerned about eating their lunch; however, Jesus used the incident of the Samaritan woman to lift their minds to a higher goal—their mission of bringing the world to Christ. His question about harvest provided a bridge from their physical concern about filling their stomachs to his loftier one of saving souls.

Jesus told them in verse 35, "Wake up and look around. The fields are already ripe for harvest." Those words certainly must have made a huge impression on the disciples when the people of the town, having believed the testimony of the woman at the well, began coming out to see and hear him in verse 39. They saw with their own eyes the harvest he had spoken of.

Using a combination of both basic questions and relationship questions, it doesn't take long to fill several pages of an Observation Chart. As you can see, the process often cycles, going back and forth between one kind of question and the other as relationship questions spawn basic questions and vice versa. I hope this chapter has helped you to understand the process well enough to work it yourself. The next step in Bible study is interpretation, which I will introduce in the next chapter.

Assignment

On the observations you have already made from John 2 using the relationship questions, write down at least ten new interpretive questions.

Step Two

How to "Know It"
A Guide to Interpretation

Chapter 6: Interpretation—
Find the True Meaning
Discover the True Truth of the Bible

When we seek to understand the meaning of our observations, we engage in *interpretation*. Interpretation may be defined as, "The process of determining the meaning of the text." The ultimate goal of interpretation is to understand what the passage means. We want to discover what the authors of the books of the Bible meant when they wrote Scripture. Each of these authors was human, but each wrote under the influence of the Holy Spirit of God. So when we discover what the human author meant, we discover what the divine author meant.

The Postmodern Error

Many people today, however, doubt that we can know what the divine author meant. Not long ago a young man said to me, "With so many interpretations of the Bible, how do I know what I am supposed to believe? It seems to me that when I read the Bible I can just believe anything I want." Today people have heard so many wildly varying interpretations of the Bible that they wonder if anyone can really know what it means, or if it really means anything that's objectively true. The confusion extends even further. Many today doubt that absolute truth even exists, or if it does, they think it's impossible to know it. This kind of doubt has affected many Christians, even those who believe in the Bible. While they are convinced that it is true, they doubt the ability of any given person to interpret its truth accurately and objectively. You hear it all the time: "If your interpretation works for you, go for it. But it speaks to me differently here. What's important to me is how I understand it." Or, "I did not get the same thought from that verse that you got. But that's okay. What's true for me may not be true for you."

For example, some religious people do not believe that Jesus Christ is the incarnate Son of God who came to the earth in human flesh. We Christians teach that he is indeed the Son of God. Obviously, both of these teachings cannot be true. There is no in-between ground, no way to synthesize opposites, no way to reconcile the two views. Either Christ is the Son of God or he is not. If he is not the Son of God, then there may be any number of possible interpretations of who he was. The Bible, however, claims that he is the Son of God. That is the major theme of the gospel of John. You can, if you wish, impose your individual "interpretation" on that book and come up with whatever alternate meaning you want it to have. But if you do this, you are not really interpreting. You are imposing your opinion and calling it interpretation. Valid interpretation seeks to discover what the text actually meant to its author.

Christians determined to follow God and know his will must reject today's popular approach to Bible interpretation. The truth of the Bible exists as a solid fact independent of how we see it. Jesus Christ lived, taught, was crucified, and rose again. That is a solid fact of history, strongly affirmed by the Bible whether or not you choose to think it's true for you. Either Christ is the Son of God or he is not. Either the Bible is objectively true or it is not. How you and I view these truths does not change their accuracy or objective validity one millimeter. Hiding behind the tired old excuse that the Bible cannot be understood objectively is laziness, cowardice, or agenda driven.

Interpretation—Find the True Meaning

Second Peter 1:20 tells us that no Scripture is of individual interpretation. It has objective meaning that needs to be discovered with humility—a willingness to accept whatever it means regardless of our preconception, theology, philosophy, or preference. It means what it means, not what I think it means or what I want it to mean. Interpretation is not constructed; it is discovered.

Second Timothy 3:16–17 says, "All Scripture is inspired by God and is useful to teach us what is true and to make us realize what is wrong in our lives. It corrects us when we are wrong and teaches us to do what is right. God uses it to prepare and equip his people to do every good work." Look at what this passage says Scripture does for us. It teaches truth, shows us right and wrong, straightens us out, points us in the right direction, and equips us to do God's will. Now, would any of this make sense if Scripture is so obscure and hard to interpret that it cannot be understood? Certainly not. To the contrary, Scripture must be understandable or it cannot perform the functions Paul claims for it in this passage.

We all share the same Bible and the same Holy Spirit. God desires that all of us know the truth he gives us in this inspired book. He intends that each of us should be able to understand it for what it means objectively, not for what it means to each of us individually.

Keys to Interpretation

The purpose of interpretation is to find out what the Bible means objectively, to find the truth it conveys so we can accept it humbly and apply it rigorously. In spite of claims to the contrary, the Bible is not really hard to understand. You don't have to be a seminary graduate, you don't have to know Greek or Hebrew, and you don't have to attend a Bible school. All these disciplines have great value and I recommend them. But they are not absolutely necessary to understanding. All of us can learn to glean the truth and meaning of the Bible. Of course, it takes study and effort. But once you know how to approach Scripture with the right method of interpretation, it becomes amazingly understandable.

Let's look at a few of the factors to consider when interpreting a Bible passage.

Metaphor

Part of interpretation is simply applying common sense. You can understand passages better if you allow language to speak in ordinary ways instead of imposing some kind of special, artificial standard for language usage in the Bible. The Bible is literature, and the same linguistic principles apply to it as to other writings. Some people fail to see this simple fact. Since they are convinced that every word of the Bible is literally true, they have trouble accepting many obvious metaphors as metaphoric. While you are right to believe the Bible is true, you must allow metaphors, similes, and analogies to be what they are and not force them to be literal. For example, when Jesus says, "I am the bread of life," does he mean that he is a loaf of ground grain mixed with yeast and baked? Of course not! He is saying metaphorically that he provides sustenance for our spiritual life just as a loaf of bread provides sustenance for our physical life. This example is too obvious to question, of course. But you would be surprised at the contrived interpretations you hear when people try to make biblical metaphors read literally.

Grammar

Not only does the Bible use metaphor, it also uses grammar. Don't worry, I'm not going to have you diagramming sentences. But we must pay attention to grammar because it often becomes a factor in accurate interpretation. Grammar involves such things as verb

Interpretation—Find the True Meaning

tenses, questions, commands, subjects, and objects. These elements determine the structure of the language, and they are important factors in determining exactly what is being said.

For example, grammar affects the interpretation of Jesus' statement, "I am the bread of life" just as much as the recognition of metaphor. Notice that he uses the "to be" verb in the present tense: "I *am* the bread of life." It is significant that he did not say, "I was the bread of life," or even "I will be the bread of life." The use of *I am* indicates the unchanging, eternal nature of Christ. It reminds us of how God identified himself to Moses at the burning bush on Mount Sinai. When Moses asked for the name of God to give Pharaoh when he asked who sent him, the only name God would give is "I AM." This use of the same term on the part of Jesus affirms his deity. He is the God who always is—the eternal sustainer of the universe and the eternal sustainer of our own lives.

History

The Bible was written in specific historical time periods. The attitudes, setting, lifestyle, and political structure of a certain time will affect the meaning of a passage. Let's consider Jesus' statement, "I am the bread of life" in its historical context. What does that tell us about how to interpret it?

The historical setting was the first century during the Roman occupation of Israel. At that time, bread was the main food source. It was not a supplement to the main meal as it is today—something to eat along with your steak, potatoes, and salad. Bread *was* the main meal. So Jesus' use of bread as the metaphor stresses his vital importance to the spiritual life of his hearers. Just as without bread they would die physically, without Jesus they would die spiritually.

If we do not properly consider metaphor, grammar, and history, we risk missing the objective meaning of the passage. When we miss objective meaning we risk the possibility that we will inadvertently impose our own meaning on it and miss the truth it intends to convey.

The Interpretive Process

So far in this book we've shown you how to set up the questions and use them to probe certain passages. We've worked through the process of making observations. Now it's time to determine what those observations mean. That's where the interpretation step begins.

But as I speak of steps, I want to make an important point before we move on. As you work your charts, don't try to maintain a rigid distinction between Observation and interpretation. The only way I can give you these methods of learning and understanding the Bible is to put them into separate steps, explaining how each works before moving on to the next. In actual practice, however, the steps will tend to blend. In time you may not even be conscious of them as separate steps because one step will merge into another as you work. For example, much of your observation has interpretation built into it. In an earlier exercise you observed that Nicodemus was a Pharisee. When you went on to ask the basic question, "What is a Pharisee?" you were really asking an interpretive question. To find the answers to such questions, you often need to do more than just observe the text because the immediate text does not provide the answer. The answer will require not mere observation; it will require interpretation. In the discussion of metaphor, grammar, and history above, no doubt you noticed that some of the information I gave you did not come directly from the Bible. The importance

Interpretation—Find the True Meaning

of bread in first-century culture, for example, must be learned elsewhere.

So, now you may ask, "How do I find the accurate answers to my interpretive questions?" You will need reference books or computer resources to find the full meanings. The answer you find will be more than just observation, it will be interpretation. For example, when you encounter the term "Pharisee" in your observation step, you could choose to maintain rigid adherence to completing that step and simply continue to make observations from the text—a Pharisee was a ruler of the Jews, a leader, a member of the synagogue, etc. But it makes more sense while you've encountered the subject of Pharisees to go on to interpretation and find out exactly what a Pharisee was. Let the steps run together and complete the process of discovery when you encounter the subject.

Interpretation builds on the foundation of observation. If you observe what the Bible says and bring all these observations together, you can interpret more accurately. The greater the quality of observation, the more accurate the interpretation. As you continue to read this book, you will notice many ideas repeated. Much of what we learned about observation will flow into interpretation. Many of the principles we use in observation work for interpretation as well.

But before we begin, you need to acquire another preliminary information-capture chart. Actually, it is more accurate to call this one an interpretation sheet instead of a chart on which to record your interpretations as you develop them. It hardly makes sense to call it a chart because it has no columns, just a heading at the top center reading, "Interpretation." Beneath that heading, also centered, you can record the passage you will be interpreting. In the space beneath, you will fill in the information you glean on that passage from the interpretation process. Later you will refer to this sheet for your interpretations of passages and words when you make your final outline.

In the next two chapters I will introduce the process of interpretation. As we move through each step, you will find your knowledge increasing steadily. You will understand not only what the author said, but also why he said it and what he meant.

Chapter 7: Let the Bible Interpret for You
Using the Bible as a Resource

No doubt you have heard preachers or Bible teachers say that the Bible explains itself. Of course, they don't mean the book starts talking to you in an audible voice as you read, saying, "Let me tell you all about what I mean here." They mean that the Bible often discusses the same or related topics in more than one place, expanding the meaning or adding nuances to it. Thus, you can understand a given passage better if you learn where to find its topic discussed in another passage.

Cross-Reference

Finding these related passages is called *cross-referencing*, which means simply following a topic or a word from one verse to another within the Bible to glean all the book has to say on the subject. Cross-referencing is only one of the tools of good interpretation, and it's the one we will start with. Later in the chapter, we will explore other interpretation tools from within the Bible, such as contexts and definitions.

The power of cross-referencing is in its authority. Since you are allowing Scripture to interpret Scripture, you can depend on the correctness of your findings. I personally find it to be one of the most enjoyable phases of Bible study, for at this stage you really begin to see the meaning of the Bible unfolding before you.

The usual method of cross-referencing is to begin with the big picture and narrow it down to specifics. You begin by looking at the questions you raised to form your observations. To record your interpretations, you need—guess what?—another chart. This chart is called the Cross-Reference Chart, and you can see a sample on page 92 or print a copy from Bonus Resources (see Appendix A, page 159).

Cross-Referencing Resources

Several resources are available to locate cross-references. Many editions or translations of the Bible have cross-references listed in a separate column beside the verses. A good example of this is the *Life Application Study Bible.* Another is the *New American Standard Bible.* Online resources are highly effective in cross-referencing because of the speed with which you can find them on the computer. A good example is Biblegateway.com, which is very attractive because all the cross-references are hyperlinked.

Another good resource for cross-referencing is your Bible concordance. A concordance is useful because sometimes the word you want to reference may not be listed in your Bible translation's cross-reference column. Another useful tool is a chain reference Bible. The original chain reference Bible that is still available on the market today is the *Thompson Chain Reference Bible.* A chain-reference Bible can be quite helpful because its elaborate marginal references and reference index in the back can help you trace a given topic throughout the entire Bible.

How to Cross-Reference

For our first cross-referencing exercise, turn again to John 3. In the first verse we have the word "Pharisee" that we've already spent a little time with, so let's start with it. We want to know what the Bible can tell us about Pharisees, so where else in the Bible is that word mentioned or discussed? I start by looking at the word in my *Life Application Study Bible.* I check the margin and find that the word is not cross-referenced. While cross-references are there, if you look them up, you'll find that the word being referenced is

"Nicodemus" and not "Pharisee." You can use that information to tell you more about Nicodemus and answer other questions on your chart. I also check the New American Standard Bible and find that there are no cross references on this verse at all.

So my next step is to turn to my Bible concordance. I look up "Pharisee" in the concordance, and there I find a list showing me all the verses in the Bible where that word appears. One helpful feature of a concordance is that it displays a few words of the phrase in which the word is used, giving you a key to what the verse is about. Since the concordance gives us many references to "Pharisee," I suggest starting with those within the book you are studying, in our case, the book of John. Then after checking the references in the book of John, look next at those in other books by the same author (John), and from those to the entire New Testament. If you do not have time to check all the references, stick with those written by the same author. It's best to let him interpret his own words.

This kind of search is considerably easier in an online resource such as Biblegateway.com. There you can choose your Bible version, type in the word you are looking for, and the search engine will bring up a list of all the verses in the Bible containing the word you want. In the case of "Pharisee," there are about one hundred instances of its use in the New Testament. On your screen, you can quickly scan those verses in the book of John and pick out the ones that give you useful information.

As you scan those verses in the book of John, you find quite a few hints about the Pharisees: They were members of a group called the "high council" (some versions use the word "Sanhedrin," John 11:47); they were sticklers for strict interpretation of the law (John 8:3); they didn't believe Jesus was the Messiah (John 9:16); and many verses show that they opposed Jesus and were out to get him. All of this is useful in building a picture of the attitudes and actions of the Pharisees. You will want to enter what is pertinent on your chart.

Following the Chain

Now we want to do an exercise showing how to cross-reference from the margin notes of a Bible. While this method is more tedious and unnecessary if you have computer resources, I include it because you may want to do your Bible study at times when you do not have access to a computer. You may have a two-hour airplane flight, or you may be sitting in the airport waiting for your flight, or in a doctor's waiting room. If you don't carry a laptop computer, then all you have is a Bible and a notepad. You can still do your Bible study if your Bible has marginal references. For this exercise I will use the New American Standard Bible since that version keys its marginal references with superscript numbers. As I noted above, that version has no marginal reference to "Pharisee," so we will follow the word "ruler" instead. This makes sense because in our earlier chart, one of our basic questions was, "Who are the rulers?"

On your Cross-Reference Chart, in the first column, write the word, *Ruler*. Now, in verse 1, printed immediately to the left of the word "ruler," notice the small superscript letter *b*. Then look in the margin horizontal to the verse and find the number 1, which indicates cross-references to verse 1. Then you find the superscript letter *b*. Beside that letter you will see the references, Luke 23:13 and John 7:26 and 48.

> | 25 ªMatt. 9:4; John 1:42, 47; 6:61, 64; 13:11
> |
> | 1 ªJohn 7:50; 19:39 ᵇLuke 23:13; John 7:26, 48
> |
> | 2 ¹Or, *attesting miracles* ªMatt. 23:7; John 3:26 ᵇJohn 2:11 ᶜJohn 9:33; 10:38; 14:10f.; Acts 2:22; 10:38
> |
> | 3 ¹Or, *from above* ªᵃ2Cor. 5:17; 1 Pet. 1:23 ᵇMatt. 19:24; 21:31; Mark 9:47; 10:14f.; John 3:5
>
> **CHAPTER 3**
>
> Now there was a man of the Pharisees, named ªNicodemus, a ᵇruler of the Jews;
>
> 2 this man came to Him by night, and said to Him, "ªRabbi, we know that You have come from God as a teacher; for no one can do these ¹ᵇsigns that You do unless ᶜGod is with him."
>
> 3 Jesus answered and said to him, "Truly, truly, I say to you, unless one is born ¹again, he cannot see ᵇthe kingdom of God."
>
> 4 Nicodemus *said to Him, "How can a man be born when he is old? He cannot enter a second time into his mother's womb and be born, can he?"

Next, on your Cross-Reference Chart, in the left column under the heading "Cross-Reference," write down Luke 23:13. Then turn to that verse and read it (here and throughout this section I am quoting from the NASB version): "And Pilate summoned the chief priests and the rulers and the people." What does this verse tell you about the rulers? What do you see that is significant to interpreting the meaning of "ruler"? We see that Pilate recognized the Pharisee rulers as leaders of the Jews. The fact that he summoned them shows that he had some kind of relationship with them and exercised authority over them. So on your chart in the "Significance" column horizontal to the reference Luke 23:13, write down, "Relationship with Pilate."

What else do we find in Luke 23:13? We have two classes of people mentioned there—not only rulers but also chief priests. So, on your chart in the "Significance" column beneath "Relationship to Pilate," you can write down, "Categories," and beneath that, "Chief Priests." What other category of ruler do we know of? Pharisees. We've already learned enough about them to know that they are a kind of Jewish ruler, so under "Categories" add "Pharisees" beneath "Chief Priests."

Now we will briefly follow the chain of references to show you how the process works. Notice in the Luke 23:13 passage the small superscript letter *a* appearing immediately at the left of the word "rulers."

---

12 ªActs 4:27

13 ªLuke 23:35; John 7:26, 48; 12:42; Acts 3:17; 4:5, 8; 13:27

¶13 And Pilate summoned the chief priests and the ªrulers and the people,
14 and said to them, "You brought this man to me as one who ªincites the people to rebellion, and behold, having examined Him before you, I ᵇhave found no guilt in this man regarding the charges which you make against Him.

Look for the corresponding *a* beside 13 in the margin, and you find a reference to Luke 23:35. Write down Luke 23:35 in the "Cross-Reference" column of your chart, then turn to the verse and read it: "And the people stood by, looking on. And even the rulers were sneering at Him, saying, 'He saved others; let Him save Himself if this is the Christ of God, His Chosen One.'" What do we learn about the rulers in this verse? They were sneering at Jesus. They had a strong disdain for him. Could this mean our speculation about why Nicodemus came to Jesus after dark was accurate? Was he fearful of what his peers would think if he were seen in the company of a person the other rulers didn't believe in and looked down on?

Notice that this verse also has a superscript letter indicating another cross-reference for the word, "ruler." When we check the reference in the margin, however, we find that it sends us back to John 3:1, which is where we started. This shows us that we have reached the end of the chain of references for this particular word, though on many other words the chain can continue much longer.

But we are not yet done with this word. When we looked at the cross-referenced verse, Luke 23:13, we followed only one of the additional references given there. Now let's go back and look at the others. Ideally, if you have the time, you should look up all the references to Luke 23:13 before you go back to John 3:1, where we started.

The next reference to Luke 23:13 is John 7:26. In the "Cross-Reference" column of your chart, write down "John 7:26," then turn to that verse and read it: "And look, He is speaking publicly, and they are saying nothing to Him. The rulers do not really know that this is the Christ, do they?" What is the significance of this passage? It's clear that the Jewish leaders were ignorant of the fact that Jesus was the Christ. The people seemed to think that they should know, and perhaps they were deliberately ignoring the obvious truth. At any rate, we can see from this passage that the rulers of the Jews did not believe that Jesus was the Christ. On your chart in the "Significance" column opposite of John 7:26, write, "Rulers didn't believe in Christ."

The next reference to Luke 23:13 is John 7:48. It reads, "No one of the rulers or Pharisees has believed in Him, has he?" What significance do you see here? This passage tells us that the Jewish rulers were not aware of any among themselves who believed in the authenticity of Jesus. Apparently, if any of them believed, they kept it to themselves. This lends support to our guess that Nicodemus was afraid to speak up and take a stance in opposition to the rest of the leaders lest he lose his high position and be expelled from the synagogue. So, in the "Significance" column of your chart opposite to John 7:48, write, "Nicodemus afraid to speak of his relationship to Jesus."

Our next reference to Luke 23:13 shows that we are not surmising at all when we interpret verse 48 as we just did above. That reference, John 12:42, reads: "Nevertheless many even of the rulers believed in Him, but because of the Pharisees they were not confessing Him, lest they should be put out of the synagogue." Our suspicions seem to be confirmed. Nicodemus was apparently one of these rulers who believed, but he kept it silent to protect his position. That, no doubt, explains why he went to Jesus after dark. The Pharisees had authority over the rulers when it came to religious matters and they could throw anyone who believed in Christ out of the synagogue. This verse also shows that Nicodemus was not alone. A number of the rulers believed in Jesus but were not admitting it.

In the "Cross-Reference" column of your chart, write John 12:42, then across from it in the "Significance" column write, "Many rulers believe in Jesus—never said so for fear of the Pharisees. Pharisees could put them out of the synagogue."

I seldom follow more than three generations of cross-references from the original. Time is usually the big factor. And I usually find that three references give me the information I need. If not, I will go further in a given case, but that's rarely necessary.

When you exhaust all further references to Luke 23:13, go back to John 3:1 and check for additional references. As it happens, the other reference for John 3:1 is John 7:48, which we've already explored. So, at this point we have exhausted the cross-references to this passage.

In the illustration on page 93 you can see an example of a Cross-Reference Chart prepared by a student. Notice that this student did go a little further than we did in the demonstration, adding three cross-references from Acts. If you have the time, going further is a fine thing to do.

Context

Like cross-referencing, considering context is another way of allowing the Bible to interpret itself. But instead of following a word or idea through the Bible, with context we stay closer to home and consider the word or verse within the *context* of the verses preceding and following it.

Context can be critically important. Many Bible study errors can be traced to the failure to consider context. By choosing verses selectively and ignoring context, you can make the Bible say anything you want. The old story goes that a man got crosswise with another member of his church, and the conflict escalated to outright hatred. With a Bible in his hand, he approached his foe and said, "I can show you that the Bible commands you to do away with yourself." He turned to Matthew 27:5, and read, "Judas…went out and hanged himself." Then he turned to Luke 10:37 and read, "Now go and do the same."

Many biblical misunderstandings and misinterpretations can be resolved by considering context. For example, I have seen students read both Paul and James on the subject of faith and works and assume that the two writers are in conflict with each other. In James 2:17 we read that "faith by itself isn't enough" (some versions say that faith without works is "dead"). Yet in Galatians 3, Paul asserts that faith, not works, is the only means to salvation. Which is it: faith or works? Do we have Scripture contradicting itself here? No, we do not. The seeming contradiction comes from isolating the verses from their contexts. When Paul speaks of faith in the book of Galatians, he relates it to salvation. Faith in Christ is our means of showing dependence on him and thus our means of accepting salvation. James, on the other hand, is not speaking of salvation, but rather of sanctification—of growing up in the faith, of living the life of a Christian. He is telling us that true faith is not merely a declaration of belief but also an attitude of trust, which involves not only what we say but also what we do. James says, in effect, "Talk is cheap. You say you have faith; prove it by what you do." Paul and James do not conflict. When you look at the context, you can see how their different emphases fit together to give us a more complete picture than either gives alone.

To show what context reveals, let's revisit John 7:48, a cross-reference passage we considered above. In the New Living Translation, that verse reads, "Is there a single one of us rulers or Pharisees who believes in him?" Apparently, if any of the Pharisees or Jewish rulers believed in Jesus, they kept it to themselves and the group as a whole did not know of it. But this verse has a fuller meaning as we read on. The assumption that there were no believers among the Jewish rulers is erroneous. In the next verse we find that there was at least one man among them who was in sympathy with Jesus. The spokesman for the Jewish leaders went on to say:

> *'This foolish crowd follows him, but they are ignorant of the law. God's curse is on them!' Then Nicodemus, the leader who had met with Jesus earlier, spoke up. 'Is it legal to convict a man before he is given a hearing?' he asked. They replied, 'Are you from Galilee, too? Search t he Scriptures and see for yourself—no prophet ever comes from Galilee!'* (John 7:49–52, NLT)

The Jewish leaders pointed out that none of the learned Pharisees believed in Jesus—just the rabble multitude that the Pharisees disdained as being too stupid to know better. At this point our friend Nicodemus's conscience must have been pricked. He stepped in with a tentative defense of Jesus, reminding his ruling peers that the law forbids judging a man until they consider in a just trial all that he says and does. But the other rulers turned angrily on Nicodemus, implying that he had taken sides with Jesus and that he had not studied prophecy carefully enough to know that the Messiah would not come from Galilee.

Notice how Nicodemus reacted to this angry accusation . . . he didn't. He kept quiet and did not reveal his nighttime meeting with Jesus. He could have told them, "Look, I personally went and talked with this man, and he is much more reasonable than you think. Here is what he told me . . ." But Nicodemus said nothing. He let the scene play out as if he had never met Jesus. We can easily surmise that Nicodemus was afraid to speak up and take a stance in opposition to the rest of the leaders lest he lose his high position and be expelled from the synagogue.

Here you see how much you can learn by reading a reference verse within its context. Enter your findings from the context on your Interpretation Sheet.

Assignment

1. Choose a word from John 1 and make a Cross-Reference Chart on it.
2. Select a passage and read the related verses before and after it. Then enter your findings on your Interpretation Sheet.

Cross-Reference Chart
(Word or Verse)

Cross-reference	Significance

Cross-Reference Chart
(Word or Verse)

Cross-reference	Significance
"Ruler"	

Luke 23:13	Relationship with Pilate
	Categories
	   Chief priest
	   Rulers

Luke 23:35	Sneered at Jesus
John 7:26	Rulers didn't believe in Christ
John 7:48	Nicodemus afraid to speak of his relationship to Jesus
John 12:42	Many rulers believe in Jesus—never said so out of fear of Pharisees. Pharisees could put them out of the synagogue.
Acts 3:17	Peter points out "rulers" acted in ignorance concerning Christ just as he did.
Acts 4:5, 8	Two more categories: elders and scribes. After 500 believed, the rulers and others gathered with the high priest asked Peter questions.
Acts 13:27	Paul exhorted Jewish leaders in the synagogue. He says neither the people nor their rulers recognized Him or His teachings.

Chapter 8: Search Outside the Bible
Using Extra-biblical Resources

The Bible interprets itself, but much information necessary to gain a thorough knowledge of the book must come from other sources. Through the centuries, scholars relying on historical texts, archaeology, and the writings of early Christians have constructed volumes of excellent information on the Bible that you can access through books and computer resources. In this chapter we will consider some of these resources and give you brief overviews on their uses.

For our demonstration on how to do interpretation, we will continue to use John 3, this time verses 1–10. So on your Interpretation Sheet, record that reference beneath your heading. You will fill in the information you glean on that passage in the space beneath it. Later you will refer to this chart for your interpretations of passages and words when you make your final outline.

Definitions

The most effective way to interpret a word from the Bible—to know the meaning of it—is to look it up in a dictionary. I suggest that you start with a general dictionary. Often ordinary dictionaries will give you the Bible definition of the word you are researching. Dictionaries also give you the background of the word, including its origin and various usages.

Another source for definitions is a Bible dictionary. Usually a Bible dictionary will give you a more expanded biblical definition than a general dictionary. A good Bible dictionary gives you not only the definition and the background of a word, but also its Old and New Testament usages.

It's good when looking up words in dictionaries to also check out their opposites, or antonyms. Often opposites help define each other. For example, when looking up *love*, also look up *hate*. When looking up *Pharisee*, also look up *Sadducee*. I find it helpful to look up related words as well. When looking up *teacher*, also look up *education*, and even *Jewish education*. Following such trails will both expand and sharpen your knowledge of your subject.

Bible Translations and Paraphrases

The next resources to consider are translations of the Bible other than the one you customarily use. You note that in our study above I have crossed back and forth between the different versions. Comparing alternate wording is often useful in giving you a fresh view of the subject and opening your eyes to expanded interpretations. I suggest looking at two or three alternate translations and paraphrases. Many good paraphrases are on the market now, and one of the most popular and useful is *The Message*. I offer one word of caution about the use of paraphrases: Don't base your doctrine on them. Paraphrases are often done by one person, and as good as they may be, they will inevitably reflect his viewpoints. For doctrine, always go to a good translation put together by a committee of respected scholars.

Reference Books

Today many other resources are available for looking up words, ideas, Bible history, and information about life, thinking, and attitudes in Bible times. I have already mentioned some of these book categories, but I will list a few of them again below. They include study Bibles, word studies, atlases, encyclopedias, commentaries, and topical books. These materials give us the scholarly insights of experts and observations of people who have spent a lifetime of research and study into subjects you and I may never be able to explore for ourselves. Often such books can supply wide-ranging information that is immensely helpful in bringing understanding and clarity to Bible words or passages.

I have encountered many people who insist that they will use nothing in their study but the Bible itself. They believe that if one is sufficiently "led by the Spirit" he or she will not need to depend on other books to understand the Bible. I believe their viewpoint to be erroneous, however, because the Bible itself makes it clear that God has given us teachers, as well as other Christians with specialized gifts designed to build up the church and strengthen members. Any time we listen to a preacher in a church or a Bible teacher in a classroom or small group setting, we are, in effect, "going outside the Bible" to learn what someone else has to say about what the Bible says. It is no different when a teacher pours his or her knowledge into a book for us to read instead of giving it to us orally. Over the centuries, many devout and dedicated Christians have compiled written resources that can be highly valuable to us in learning more about the truth of the Bible.

Following are several types of extra-biblical helps that you may find useful.

Study Bibles

A study Bible is one of the most useful study tools you can own. Study Bibles contain such wide-ranging information that you would have no way of knowing unless you are a Bible teacher or a serious student. A good study Bible may replace many of the types of reference books listed below. Many study Bibles include a brief Scripture commentary, introductions to Bible books and summaries of them, charts, maps, graphs, sidebars, textual footnotes, chain references, dictionaries, concordances, and other informational help that may often deflect the need to turn to other resources. Most study Bibles are designed around a given theme. For example, there are men's study Bibles, women's study Bibles, teen study Bibles, application study Bibles, etc. Others are based on such things as prophecy, spiritual warfare, or evangelism. New ones appear on the market regularly. You must examine them for yourself and choose the one that best fits your needs.

Let me briefly show you an example of a study Bible in use. In the *Life Application Study Bible*, we can go to the master index in the back and look up a word. Let's use one we're already familiar with—*Pharisee*. In addition to giving us a list of verses where there is a note about the Pharisees, the index tells us there's a chart about Pharisees on a particular page. Turning to that page, we see that the chart has a brief definition of both Pharisees and Sadducees, along with two columns showing both the positive and negative characteristics of each group. Within the definition and the two lists, we get a clear picture of who the Pharisees were, what they believed, and how they behaved. From these descriptions we see more clearly why they opposed Jesus so vehemently. Information you glean from a study Bible can be placed on your Interpretation Sheet.

Word Studies

Serious students or Bible teachers will find a word study book useful for the detailed information it provides about given words. Not only do you get a definition, you also get the cultural background of the word, its usage in that culture, its origin, and its history. My own preference for word study books is *Wuest* and *Vine*. Your local bookstore clerk will be happy to introduce you to others.

Atlases

A Bible atlas or even a general atlas is useful in helping you to picture the movements and travels of Bible characters and peoples. For example, in studying John 4 where we're told that Jesus and his disciples had to leave Judea and travel through Samaria to get to Galilee, an atlas will help you to visualize their journey by showing you the relationship of the three geographical areas and the miles they had to travel. You can understand much more about Paul's hardships on his journeys if you study his travels on a first-century map. Atlases are also useful in showing the changes in political boundaries over the centuries. A map of Palestine at the time of its settlement by the twelve tribes of Israel is quite different from the same area under Roman occupation in the time of Christ. Atlases can show you the scope of the great empires involved in Bible history—Egyptian, Assyrian, Babylonian, Persian, Greek, and Roman.

Sometimes a map may provide the essential key to unlocking your understanding of a Bible passage or book. You can hardly get a clear understanding of the book of Joshua, for example, without a map. Only by referring to a map as you read of the conquest of Canaan can you appreciate the brilliance of Joshua's battle strategy. World War II general Douglas MacArthur and Israeli general Moshe Dayan both admired General Joshua and studied his plan for defeating the Canaanites. You can bet that as these men read Joshua; they traced his military movements on good maps.

All study Bibles, and even many editions of the Bible, contain most of the maps you will need. Teachers and serious students, however, may want to consider an atlas as an additional resource for more in-depth and detailed geographical information.

Encyclopedias

Both general encyclopedias, such as *Encyclopedia Britannica*, and Bible encyclopedias are helpful research tools. They can give you broad information on Bible history, geography, culture, people, artifacts, and archaeology. Naturally, a Bible encyclopedia is more focused and detailed on Bible subjects than a general encyclopedia. Again, a good study Bible can provide you with much of what you will find in a Bible encyclopedia, though, of course, not with the same depth and detail.

Commentaries

A Bible commentary is exactly what the term implies. It is a Bible scholar's comments explaining the meaning of Bible passages. Commentaries can be in-depth, verse-by-verse, multi-volume works or single-volume commentaries on the entire Bible treating the basic themes of chapters and hitting certain highlighted verses. One staple feature of study Bibles is that they all have a running commentary accompanying the text.

Of course, any time we use a commentary, we must remember that we are reading the viewpoint of a single author. These authors are human and capable of erring just as we are. We must always have our senses alert to compare what commentaries teach with what we observe for ourselves in the Bible.

Topical Books

Christian bookstores are filled with books on any topic you want to learn about in depth. You can buy scholarly or popularly written books on subjects like justification, redemption, salvation, sanctification, Christian living, God, the Holy Spirit, Jesus, or you name it. If your focus in Bible study is a particular topic, check with your local bookstore for the best resources available.

Computer Resources

Several times in this book, I have alluded to the computer resources now available to Bible students, both online and in software you can install on your own computer. Many of these computer resources can replace most of the books I listed above. An excellent example of an online resource is the one I've already mentioned, Biblegateway.com, which is superb for finding specific Scriptures and linking references. This amazing resource has the complete text of every major Bible translation on the market today. And by just typing in your Scripture reference or a word or two, you can use it as a concordance or to look up the text of any verse in the Bible in any version. And with computer resources the response is immediate. Not only do you save the time of turning pages, you also save the time involved in writing the passage down. You can merely copy it and paste it into your document.

A fine example of Bible software you can install on your computer is iLumina Gold. This program can replace virtually every book I've mentioned above. It has a Bible dictionary, a Bible encyclopedia, the complete text of the Bible in four versions with several ways of accessing it, Bible study helps, charts, maps, and commentaries. In addition it has many visual features, including photos, illustrations, animated clips of many Bible incidents, and archaeological information.

To show you only one example of what iLumina can do for you, let's use it to look up the word *Pharisee*. From the home page, you go to the encyclopedia. Click on the "All articles" box at the bottom of the page, and you get both a list of topics and a box to type in the word you're searching for. Type in "Pharisee," and instantly a thorough article on Pharisees and Sadducees comes up with the information divided into the following subheads: Pharisees in the

New Testament, Origins of the Pharisees, and Basic Characteristics of the Pharisees. Then the same information on the Sadducees follows. If that's more information than you want, a summary box at the right of the page gives you the "Fast Facts" about the Pharisees and compares them with the Sadducees. All this information is placed right before your eyes in a matter of seconds.

When you get the definitions you want, copy and paste them on your Interpretation Sheet and document your sources.

Building Interpretation on the Foundation of Observation

To show you how interpretation builds on observation, I refer you back to our observations on the contrasts between Jesus and the Samaritan woman in John 4 that we discovered in chapter 5 of this book. In the observation process, we asked our basic questions and our relationship questions and made several observations, from which I made the simple chart on page 63. Now as you enter the interpretation step, you will go one step further than simple observation. You will ask of these observed differences between Jesus and the Samaritan woman the questions that we raised in chapter 5 that could not all be answered by observation: "What do these differences mean? How do they affect relationship and communication? Do they create barriers, or are they insignificant?" In the culture of first-century Palestine, all these differences were significant, and each would create a barrier between them, even to the point of making any kind of communication at all highly unlikely. To uncover these barriers, you will want to go back to the question, "What?" Look at each difference you observed and ask, "What barrier would this difference create between Jesus and the Samaritan woman?"

Here you need to know more about the details of first-century culture than the Bible gives. You will need some of the external helps listed above to answer these questions. A Bible encyclopedia, a study Bible, a Bible study computer program, or online Bible sites can give you thorough information that will help you understand all the barriers between Jesus and the Samaritan woman and why they existed. Following are a few facts that I gleaned from resources such as these.

> *1. The fact that the woman was a blatant sinner and Jesus was sinless created a **moral** barrier. The Jews would never stoop to socialize with an adulterer or a prostitute.*

> *2. The fact that she was a woman and he was a man created a **social** barrier. In Jewish culture of that time men and women did not mix socially even in public, much less in private. That is why we read in verse 27 that when the disciples returned from her errand, they were astounded that Jesus had been speaking with a woman.*

> *3. The fact that the woman was a Samaritan and Jesus was a Jew created a **racial** barrier. The Jews held the Samaritans in low esteem, regarding them as an impure race of Jewish blood mixed with Assyrian and other exiled races, and would have nothing to do with them.*

> *4. Being a Samaritan meant that this woman was of the Samaritan religion, which the Jews saw as a corruption of their own Judaism. The Samaritans*

*used only the first five books of the Old Testament as their Bible. They did not worship at Jerusalem, as all Jews did, but rather at Mount Gerizim in their own country. This tampering with Scripture and changes to worship caused the Jews to hate the Samaritans obsessively. Thus, there was a **religious** barrier.*

*5. The woman lived in Samaria, a country which Jews disdained since its decimation and resettlement by the Assyrians seven centuries before. So, with their separate nationalities, the woman and Jesus also faced a **political** barrier.*

Expanding the chart on page 63, I added a column to the right showing the meaning of the differences, or the interpretations I found from external sources.

Are you impressed with what we've gleaned so far? Many students are continually surprised at what the Bible will reveal to you if you simply ask the right questions and reach for a little outside interpretive help.

Differences		
Woman	Jesus	Barrier
Adulteress	Son of God, Rabbi	Moral
Woman	Man	Social
Samaritan	Jew	Racial
Samaritan religion	Judaism	Religious
From Samaria	From Judea	Political

The Goal: Interpretation

The ultimate purpose in using all these resources is to gain a greater understanding of the meaning of the Bible. That requires not only making observations on what the Bible says, but interpreting what it says—putting meaning to the words and events that will give you a thorough knowledge of the background, context, and concepts.

As I have shown you in this book so far, I do recommend starting with the Bible first. Let the book interpret itself as much as it will. Get all the meaning you can by asking questions of the verse under consideration itself and record your observations. Then start linking references and looking at the passage in its context. But you will come to a point where the passage raises more questions than mere observation can answer. You will need outside resources to give you the necessary interpretation.

For example, when you read in Nehemiah 1:11 of Nehemiah being a cup-bearer to the emperor, what does that tell you? Was he a mere lowly servant? Or was cup-bearer an important position? The text itself gives you hints at the answer, but it takes an outside source to provide the results of historical research to show you that cup-bearer was a high position in the culture of the ancient Persian empire. This kind of information adds immeasurably to your understanding of Nehemiah, but it's not available from the Bible itself. Yes, start first with the Bible and always come back to the Bible. But don't hesitate to engage the use of outside resources to broaden your understanding.

As you look at some of these resources, you will find that outlines of Bible books and passages are already available in many of them. At this point you might reasonably raise the question: "Why should I go to all the trouble of constructing my own outlines and charts when I can get this information so easily from these resources?" Two reasons come to mind immediately. First, you want your material to be your own. If you depend solely on the work of others without doing your own digging, the knowledge does not imbed itself so deeply. When you do the work—ask the questions, follow references, look up definitions, dig for background information—the knowledge sticks. It's yours. You remember it and can recall it much easier. This kind of recall and embedded knowledge is especially valuable if you are a Bible teacher. Your presentations will be richer and more from the heart. Also, you will have a great advantage when students ask questions. You can draw from the well of your personal resources and give accurate and useful answers.

Second, when you dig for your own information and make your own charts and outlines, your teaching will be unique. You will have insights that no one else has. You will put together your material in a way that no one else does. Your teaching will be fresh and creative. It will not be dull and dry stuff you find in a book and parrot to your class; it will be invigorating and inspiring to others.

Of course, you must rely on the work of others who have gone before you. It would be foolish not to do that. But by drawing from many sources, you assemble your knowledge in a way different from any other and that kind of freshness will be apparent when you teach. As the old saying goes, "Steal from one source and we call it plagiarism. Steal from several and we call it creativity."

Assignment

1. Find a key word in John 1 and define it. Place your definition on your Interpretation Sheet.
2. Read a selected section of John 1 in two translations and a paraphrase. Record any interpretive insights you glean on your Interpretation Sheet.
3. Using an encyclopedia or a computer Bible resource, look up the word you defined above and record your significant findings on your Interpretation Sheet.

Chapter 9: Your Final Product
Outlining Your Bible Study Findings

If you have made all your preliminary charts and completed the assignments in this book, your notebook probably bulges with several pages of material, each brimming with hard-won information. This information, useful as it may be, is not yet in a useful order. You may have entries about culture on pages 1, 2, 8, and 13, while word definitions are scattered randomly throughout. Your notes and charts sparkle with gems of knowledge, but at this point it's all a hodgepodge, entered as you found it. It lacks logical order.

The next step, then, is the obvious and natural one. We take all this material and organize it into a logical and useful order, creating appropriate headings as we go. The result will enable you to retain and recall your material with greater clarity and teach it more effectively.

Many people who want to be good Bible students don't have the knack for organizing material into an outline. I encourage you to try it first, but if you have trouble finding a logical order, don't hesitate to find a model to copy. Many of the resources we introduced in the previous chapter provide outlines of Bible material. Bible dictionaries give excellent examples for outlining the meanings of specific words. Study Bibles give outlines of books of the Bible. There's nothing wrong with using these outlines to guide you as you arrange your own material.

Passage Outline

The first step in outlining is to determine what portion of Scripture you want to outline. If you intend to outline the entire book of John, for example, you have taken on quite a task and I suggest breaking it down into individual chapters first. In fact, you may prefer to break down the chapters into sections. This often makes more sense than outlining an entire chapter because many chapters may contain more than one major subject or theme. One way to determine what to outline is to go by the section divisions the publishers placed within each chapter. This method gives you a head start because the publisher has already given these chapter sections their own headings.

You may choose to add sub-outlines as addendums to your passage outline. These outlines, for example, could be of words within the passage that have enough significance to warrant exploration and individual study. This type of outlining will be especially useful to teachers. I will show you a sample of word outlining later in this chapter, but first we will tackle the task of passage outlining.

The process is not as hard as you may think. In fact the passage itself will dictate to you the points of an outline. Those points should develop along the natural progression of the passage. Before I begin with a demonstration, let me give you a couple of general principles to help you in outlining: (1) Never try to force a topic into an outline that you do not find within the passage, either explicitly or implicitly, as a result of your cross-reference or extra-biblical exploration; (2) As you construct your outline, you may use the chapter or section titles from your charts as the titles in your outline.

As an illustration of how to work the process, I will use John 1:1–18. In reviewing my observation charts, I find that I have listed four major points that emerged from my study of this passage. My first point comes from my observations of verses 1–5, in which I noted that these verses identify Christ as the Word who was God and with God from the beginning and who created the world. So, on my outline I place as my first heading, "The Word—The Uncreated Creator." For my next heading, I use my observation about John the Baptist from verses 6–8: "Forerunner of the Word." My third major division comes from verses 9–13: "Results of the Word Made Flesh." Then my fourth and last division is verses 14–18, which produces the heading, "Characteristics of the Word Made Flesh."

I consult my Observation Chart and Interpretation Sheet for subjects to serve as subdivisions under these four major divisions. Under the first major division I find material for three subdivisions:

> I. The Word—The Uncreated Creator (John 1:1–5)
>   A. Eternal existence
>   B. Eternal source
>   C. Eternal manifestation

Now I look for logical topics in my charts that should be placed beneath these subdivisions. I find material from my observations and interpretations on the divine nature that will go logically beneath "Eternal existence," so I place it there. For item B, "Eternal source," I find that I have gleaned information showing Christ to be the source of everything made as well as of life itself. So under the subheading, "B. Eternal source," I place "Material world" and "Life." I search my charts further and find that I have no additional material for "Eternal manifestation," so I leave that topic intact without subdivisions.

Next I look at the second major division of the passage, "Forerunner of the Word." I consult my charts for information that would go under this title. Here I find that a basic question prompts the answer I need. "Who was the forerunner of the Word?" I had noted the answer from verse 6: the forerunner was John the Baptist, a man sent by God. So on my outline as subtopic 1 under "II. Forerunner of the Word," I write, "A. John the Baptist: Man sent by God." I find no further subtopics for this item, so I look again at my charts.

I find another basic question: "Why?" "Why was John sent by God?" The question addresses the purpose of John's mission. So on my outline as the second subtopic under "Forerunner of the Word," I write, "B. Purpose." I continue to consult my charts for further information and answers, and I find two entries that explain John's purpose in my notes on verses 7 and 8. "He came to tell about the light," and "so that everyone might believe." So I enter these two items on my outline as subtopics 1 and 2 under "Purpose."

I think we have gone far enough with this demonstration to show you how the process of making a passage outline works. On page 118 at the end of this chapter you can see the entire outline as I completed it. You can see additional samples of passage outlines in Bonus Resources (see Appendix A on page 159 for information) The important thing to remember is to begin with the big idea, then divide it up into subtopics by finding information in your Observation Charts and Interpretation Sheet that fit naturally under each category and subcategory. Keep dividing the major topics into subtopics until you have found the natural places in your outline for all your useful information.

Here are a couple of cautions about outlining. First, when you create a heading based on a certain set of verses, all the subdivided information you place under that heading must be information derived from those verses. For example, in my demonstration outline my first heading, "The Word—The Uncreated Creator," covers verses 1–5. All my subheadings under that heading break down or elaborate on these five verses. I would not use material in these subtopics that strays from this section of Scripture because to do so would lead me into irrelevant areas and my outline would lose focus and become hard to understand or remember.

Second, never list a subtopic under a heading unless you have at least two of them. In other words, never place information under a heading as subtopic 1 unless you also have a subtopic 2. If you have only one topic to go under a heading, just enter it under the heading without a letter or number indicating a division. That is a primary principle of good outlining.

Word Study Outline

As an auxiliary to your passage outline, you may find it worthwhile for your own study or for teaching purposes to create an outline based on an important key word in your passage. You decide for yourself how detailed you want your outline to be. The example on page 119 at the end of this chapter is an outline of a single word.

To show you how the outline process works when applied to a word, I will walk you through the construction of a word outline. This outline is based on the word "water" which we found in John 3:5. I chose this outline that I did several years ago because of its simplicity. Frankly, it is simple because I remember that I ran out of time and knew I could not finish it, so I completed only the cross-reference stage. Now it seems that my failure to complete the chart may have been providential. It is perfect to provide a simple demonstration of the process without getting bogged down in too much detail. Here is how I proceeded.

I went to my cross-reference chart and studied what I had recorded there. I found that all my material on "water" could be categorized under four basic headings: (1) water as a natural liquid in the physical world, (2) water as a metaphor for the Word, (3) water as a metaphor for the Spirit, and (4) water in reference to becoming born again. I simplified these four categories into the following one- or two-word statements: (1) Water, (2) Word, (3) Spirit, (4) Born Again. Next I looked at all the cross-references I had entered on my chart and determined which of my four categories they supported. After making these determinations, I sorted them accordingly and placed each under its proper heading.

Simply placing these Scripture references under their appropriate headings, however, was not quite enough to give me a strong outline with a continual thread of meaning I could retain and teach. So I looked at each verse to find an essential meaning I could capture in four words or less. You can see the result on the previous page.

Of course, had I gone on and added material from my Interpretation Sheet, my outline would have expanded greatly. It is likely, however, that the basic form of the outline would remain intact. The additional interpretive information could easily find a natural home under the categories already listed. The Arabic number entries would increase, and likely the capital letter entries as well. And it's even possible that I would have found new Roman numeral categories. Stay flexible. The important essential of your final outline is that it organizes all your research, observations, definitions, and interpretations in a way that you can remember them and/or teach them.

Printed in Appendix A on page 159 of this book is information regarding Bonus Resources that can be accessed on-line to obtain additional examples of word outlining. These fine samples of student outlines will show you how word outlines look with information from all your charts included.

A Quick Review

With this chapter we complete the process of Bible study for the purpose of knowing content and interpretation. Before we go on to the next major step, let's take a quick overview of what we've learned. In the points below, notice how with each step we move from the general to the specific, going deeper and becoming more detailed with each move. This method keeps what you learn in context, helping you to group and organize the material logically for greater clarity and easier focus.

Chapter Titles. Chapter titles are the big handles to help us grasp and recall the content of each chapter. We captured chapter titles at the top of each column of our Title Chart.

Paragraph Titles. We titled the paragraphs within each chapter as smaller handles to help us grasp the content of each section of the chapter. We captured paragraph titles in the column below the appropriate chapter title on our Title Chart.

Observation. Next we engaged in the process of simple observation to learn how to see the content of a passage. As aids to observation, we applied the six basic or "surfacer" questions: who? what? when? where? how? why? Then we asked the twelve relationship questions to further aid our observation. We recorded our observations on an Observation Chart. In observation we were little concerned with what a passage means; at this point, we were primarily interested in seeing what is there.

Interpretation. In this step we looked at the basic principles of interpretation before beginning to seek the meanings of the observations we recorded in our observation step. The process of interpretation led us into the next two major steps involved in finding these answers—cross-referencing Bible passages and researching outside sources.

Cross-Referencing. This was our first step into interpretation—seeking the meaning behind our observations. We looked for answers from the Bible, learning to follow references until we found what the Bible had to say in other places about the subject in question. We also considered *context* as a means of determining what the Bible itself had to say on a given subject. We recorded our answers on a Cross-Reference Chart.

Extra-biblical Research. The next step in the interpretation process was to go outside the Bible and find answers to our interpretation questions by researching other resources. These included general dictionaries, Bible dictionaries, concordances, study Bibles, encyclopedias, Bible encyclopedias, commentaries, topical books, atlases, word studies, online resources, and computer software. We entered our findings on an Interpretation Sheet.

Outlining. The culmination of all our Bible study and chart making was our outline. The outline organized the material we gleaned into a logical form we can use as a teaching or study resource.

The entire Bible study process I've introduced here is designed to help you understand the content and meaning of the Bible. Of course, as I've said, the resulting outline is a fine tool for further study, memory, and teaching. But I am convinced that the process that produces this outline—the reading, digging, referencing, thinking, charting, researching, and outlining—has value within itself. The whole process puts you deeply into the Word. As you work, you begin to see things and have insights you never had before. You see the progression of thought, how things fit together, relationships between books, doctrines, Bible people, and histories that you have never seen before. Even if you never touch your outline again, you now have lodged solidly in your mind a new understanding and appreciation of God's message to you.

Assignment

1. Find a key word in John 4, and from your charts, make a word outline.
2. Look at your charts and find the chapter or section of a chapter on which you made the most complete notes. Do a passage outline on this section.

Witness of the Word Made Flesh
(John 1:1–18)

I. The Word—The Uncreated Creator (1–5)
    A. Eternal existence (1–2)
        1. Divine nature (1)
        2. Since the beginning (2)
    B. Eternal source of creation (2–4)
        1. Material world (3)
        2. Life (4)
    C. Eternal manifestation (light) (5)

II. Forerunner of the Word (6–8)
    A. Who? Man sent by God (6)
    B. Purpose? (7–8)
        1. Bear witness of the light (7a, 8)
        2. For all the world to believe (7b)

III. Results of the Word Made Flesh (9–13)
    A. Negative (9–11)
        1. Enlightens every man (9) BUT
        2. Rejected by men (10, 11)
            a. by world (10)
            b. by His own (11)
    B. Positive (12–13)
        1. Children of God by believing (12)
        2. Of God, not man (13)

IV. Characteristics of the Word Made Flesh (14–18)
    A. Only begotten of the Father (14)
    B. Greater rank than forerunner (15)
    C. Channel of grace and truth (16–17)
    D. Visible expression of invisible God (18)

Interpretation Outline of "Water"

I. Water
  A. Symbolic—not always literal
    1. Word (Ephesians 5:26)
    2. Eternal life (John 4:14, 7:36–39)
    3. Holy Spirit (John 7:39)
  B. Use of water: Washing (Ephesians 5:26, Hebrews 10:22)

II. Word
  A. Symbolic
    1. Seed (1 John 3:9)
    2. Sword of the Spirit (Ephesians 6:17)
  B. Use
    1. Cleanse (Ephesians 5:26, John 15:3; Psalm 119:9,10)
    2. Sanctify (John 17:17; 1 Peter 1:2; 1 Corinthians 6:11)
    3. Quickeneth (Psalm 119:50; Hebrews 4:12)
    4. Work in believer (1 Thessalonians 2:13)

III. Spirit
  A. Quickens (John 6:26)
  B. Sanctifies (1 Peter 1:2)
     The agent is the Word (John 17:17, 1 Corinthians 6:11)
  C. Gives life (John 6:63)

IV. Born again
  A. Water (John 3:5)
  B. Spirit (John 3:5)
  C. Word (1 Corinthians 4:15, James 1:18, 1 Peter 1:23; John 1:13, James 1:15)
  D. Seed (1 Peter 1:23; 1 John 3:9)

Step Three

How to "Do It"

A Guide to Application

Chapter 10: Principles of Application
Where the Rubber Meets the Road

You would think that Bible study has no downside. And, in essence, it doesn't. But because we are fallen humans, our reactions and responses to anything positive and beneficial can take a negative twist. C. S. Lewis noted that even when a Christian succeeds in achieving humility, the first reaction is often to be proud of it, thus defeating the achievement. With Bible study, that twist is often treating our increase in knowledge and understanding as an end within itself. Too easily we fall into the trap of becoming satisfied with interpretation and never get to application. But the goal of Bible study is not merely to increase head knowledge. Rather it is to learn how to apply correct principles to ourselves so we can live dedicated and sanctified lives. We want to apply what we learn to our everyday activities.

Few Bible scholars have had more knowledge of the Scriptures than Martin Luther. A Catholic monk, he pored over the Bible daily, spending hours coming to a detailed understanding of what he found in it. But did he stop there? Absolutely not. His knowledge moved him to action. Scripture convinced him that many of the practices of his church were wrong. He put his reputation on the line and his life in danger when he nailed to the door of the Wittenburg church a list of ninety-five errors that needed to be corrected. Later, when the events following this act placed him on trial before the emperor, he was commanded to recant the "heresy" he had learned in his studies—that salvation was by God's grace alone. But Luther faced the emperor and boldly asserted, "I cannot recant. My conscience is held captive to the Word of God."

History tells us of many other Christians who were motivated by their knowledge of the Bible to apply it and do great things for the Lord. Men like John Huss, the Bohemian reformer who was burned at the stake for his convictions; or the Englishman John Wycliffe, who was martyred for his faith as he translated the Bible into the language of the people; or of John Knox, whose passion for evangelism led him to fall to his knees and cry, "O God, give me Scotland or I die!"

In each case, these men's knowledge of Scripture led them to dedicated action. Knowledge is meaningless without application. The purpose of the Bible is to show us how to live as members of God's kingdom. Jesus himself urged us to build not just our knowledge, but also our very lives on his Word. In Matthew 7:24–27 we read,

> *Anyone who listens to my teaching and follows it is wise, like a person who builds a house on solid rock. Though the rain comes in torrents and the floodwaters rise and the winds beat against that house, it won't collapse because it is built on bedrock. But anyone who hears my teaching and ignores it is foolish, like a person who builds a house on sand. When the rains and floods come and the winds beat against that house, it will collapse with a mighty crash.*

Clearly, listening to Jesus' teachings is not enough. Obeying them is what makes us wise and gives our lives unshakable stability like a house built on a solid rock foundation.

As we have seen so far in this book, the Bible contains a tremendous store of knowledge. It's a lot to learn—a formidable task even if one devotes a lifetime of study to it. But that should not discourage us if we realize that God understands our weaknesses and limitations. He does not expect the impossible of us. He merely expects us to follow the light that we have. We learn what we can and apply it, whether it is much or little. The Lord wants us to be mature, of course, but he knows it doesn't happen overnight. Growth is a process that takes time. He will meet us where we are, and he will help us take any size step we're capable of taking toward applying his words to our lives.

In some cases Scripture application is clear and uncomplicated. For example, in the commandment, "You must not commit adultery" (Exodus 20:14), the application is right there on the surface for all to see clearly. No digging is needed. No shades of gray, no need to go searching for various personal applications. Simply read and obey. In other passages, however, while the truth may be clear, often the application is not. We must have a way of probing the passage to seek applications meaningful to our lives. As probing tools for this purpose, I have developed seven questions one can ask of any Scripture. These questions will help you uncover the applicable truths of any passage and find the ways it can apply to you.

The Seven Application Questions

To apply what I learn from my Bible study, I place before me all my charts and outlines on the Scripture I have been exploring. Then I begin asking the seven application questions. These questions help me to uncover the material from my interpretation studies that I can put into practice in my own life. As I look at the passage and my study material I ask the questions, and on my Application Sheet 1 record my answers—the applicable truths I find or my *applications*. Here are the seven questions:

1. What truths are found in this passage?

To answer this question, I study the passage and my charts and outlines to mine the text for all the applicable truths it has to offer. The number of truths you find in a given passage will vary, of course. The important thing is to ask the question rigorously to be sure you find everything that might be there. Of course, there's no way for me to give you a specific number of truths you should find. That will depend on the passage, the length of it, and the effectiveness of your exploration. But to give you a general idea, in a passage like John 3:1–10, you may come up with three to five applications in a normal study and possibly ten or more in a more concentrated lengthy study. I had one student who found thirty-six applications in the first eight verses of John 3 (see Appendix A on page 159 to access this example in Bonus Resources).

Looking at John 3:1–10, do any truths jump out at you? What do you see in Christ's statement that one must be born again to see the kingdom of God? That's a truth. One must be born again. So you can record this as a truth on your Application Sheet.

2. How does this truth apply to my life? At work? In my neighborhood? At home? In my nation?

Now you try to apply to your own life the truths you listed from question one. Does this truth apply at work? In your neighborhood? At home with your family? In your nation? Does it affect your activity? Your outlook?

Pursuing our example from question one, how does the truth, "You must be born again," apply to your life? How are you different if you are born again? Does it affect the way you see the world? What is that effect? Does it affect the way you live your life with your coworkers, your family, or your neighbors? Write out your answer in fair detail.

3. In view of this truth, what specific changes should I make in my life?

The idea behind the metaphor of being born again obviously means one becomes a new person, subject to new authorities. This question forces you to examine yourself to determine whether your life reflects that dramatic change. Are you still acting like the person you were before you were born again? Can your family, friends, and coworkers tell any difference? Do you really make all your decisions now by the standard of Christ, your new Master? Or do you still see yourself as being in charge of your own life? Be rigorous and ruthless in these uncomfortable explorations. That's the purpose, isn't it—to force you to look at problem areas you may have ignored so you can make the necessary changes in your life?

4. How do I propose to carry out these changes?

List all the ways you can think of to make changes in your life that will reflect the fact of your new birth. Maybe you need to avoid certain situations. Maybe you need to get a habit under control or your temper tamed. How do you propose to do that? Do you need an accountability partner? Will counting to three before you respond keep your tongue in check? Come up with real solutions. As you can see, these questions are relentless in their probe. They are designed to not let you off the hook. They force you not only to look and recognize your weaknesses but also to consider steps for taking action on them.

I remember when I was doing my Application Sheet on John 4. One of the basic truths I listed was to "Worship God in Spirit and Truth." As I studied worship in my observation and interpretation steps, I found that one way to worship is to help other people in Christ's name. One act of worship is to minister to others. When I came to the application question, "What changes should I make in my life?" it struck me that I was not in the habit of going out of my way to help people. So my change was to become one who made it a point to help others. At that time, I lived in the mountains near San Bernardino. In the hot summers those mountain roads often cause cars to overheat, and it's not uncommon to find several cars with radiators steaming parked on the highway shoulders. Since I often traveled that road myself, I realized that providing water for these stranded motorists would be a perfect opportunity to "worship" by helping others.

So, what did I write down as my answer to the question, "How do I propose to make this change?" I wrote, "Buy two five-gallon containers, fill them with water, and keep them in my trunk." I followed up on my solution, and the rest of the story is this: As a result of my Scripture application process, I have been able to witness to several grateful motorists along that highway. I shared a better kind of water than just H_2O.

5. What is my personal prayer regarding the application of this truth?

Let the tremendous power of prayer come to your aid as you apply these truths. Ask God for strength, wisdom, and courage to apply it successfully and to his glory. If a struggle is involved, lay it out honestly. I strongly suggest that you write out that prayer for two reasons. First, the act of writing sort of "incarnates" your thought. Rather than the prayer being mere fleeting words in your head, you have it as a tangible entity in the physical world. That makes it somehow seem more real and you will take it more seriously. Second, with the prayer written down, you can refer to it again and pray it at will.

Principles of Application

6. What verse (or verses) of Scripture could I memorize to best summarize this truth?

Committing a Bible passage to memory is the best way I know of embedding a truth deeply in your heart. Look at your Cross-Reference Chart and see if you listed a verse that encapsulates the truth you are dealing with. Often the best verse for memorizing may be the very one you are studying. One possible verse to memorize that drives home the "born again" principle from John 3 is 2 Corinthians 5:17: "This means that anyone who belongs to Christ has become a new person. The old life is gone; a new life has begun!"

7. What illustration can I develop that will help me retain this truth and communicate it to others? (A story, a poem, a graphic, a cartoon, or a drawing, for example.)

No doubt you've noticed that when sermons, lessons, or books have vivid illustrations to emphasize their points, you remember them better. In fact, I sometimes remember the illustrations in a preacher's sermon even when I forget the point. And, of course, the illustrations bring me back to the point. That's the whole point of illustrations. They make the truth vivid. They give it "flesh," you might say, so that you can relate to it better.

Your illustration might be a brief story, a poem, a graphic, a cartoon, or a drawing. One student, wanting to illustrate her place in the body of Christ, drew an outline of a body, representing Christ, or the church, and filled it with little stick drawings of many people. She marked one of these stick figures as herself (see illustration at right).

Illustration:
The Body of Christ

How would you illustrate our truth in John 3 about the need to be born again? You might write a brief story of a man who had a diseased, dying heart and desperately needed a transplant. When a healthy donor became available, he got the heart and it rejuvenated him completely. The healthy heart gave him new life. He was no longer dying. He felt that his life was starting anew, as if he had just been reborn. If writing prose is not your talent, tell the story in a poem, or draw it as a picture or a graphic. Be creative and use your best abilities to come up with some way to embody your applicable truth in an illustration.

At the end of this chapter on pages 137–139 is a sample Application Sheet created by one of my students using these seven questions. (See Appendix A on page 159 to access additional application samples in Bonus Resources.)

Application and Witnessing

Equally important to applying scriptural truths to your own life is knowing them well enough to recall when witnessing to others. Knowing the right example from the Bible can be of immense help in relating the Bible directly to their needs and situations. John 3 has several points of contact that you might find useful in creating an opening. For example, let's say you are talking with a Muslim cleric. You say to him, "Let me show you what Jesus said to a religious leader." Then you open to him the conversation between Jesus and Nicodemus in John 3. Or suppose you are talking to a state representative or a city councilman. You remember that Nicodemus was a political leader, so you show this person what Jesus said to Nicodemus.

Application of Scripture can help you immensely in witnessing. Remember in chapter five where we showed how Jesus witnessed to the Samaritan woman? First, he offered her something desirable—water that would quench her thirst forever. Second, he told her what prevented her from tasting this blessing—the immorality in her life. Third, he told her of God's plan for worship—how to establish a relationship with him. And fourth, he challenged her faith when he told her who he was. The question was, in essence, "Will you believe or not?"

Notice how closely Jesus' conversation with that woman parallels the "Four Spiritual Laws" used by Campus Crusade for Christ. The first spiritual law offers something desirable: *God loves you and offers a wonderful plan for your life.* Most evangelism techniques don't start on this positive note. They often begin by telling the person that he or she is a sinner. That's true, of course, but it's not likely to produce a positive response. No one likes to be accused—especially at the opening of a conversation. The word for *gospel* in Greek is *eugelion*, and it means "good news." But telling a person, "You are a sinner condemned to hell," is hardly good news.

Most people are looking for two things that are lacking in many lives today. The first is love, and the second is meaning. If you offer this to people, they will likely respond as the Samaritan woman did to Christ's offer of living water. They will want it. The offer will be *good news* to them.

Notice that after offering the good news to the woman, Jesus then told her why she could not experience it. She was living a life of immorality. Her sin kept her from God and thus from experiencing his living water. The second spiritual law tells us the same thing. It tells us why we cannot experience the first law. *Man is sinful and separated from God.* We can't experience God's love or follow our purpose because the barrier of our sin prevents it.

Next, Jesus showed the woman how the barrier of sin could be overcome: by a relationship with God. The third spiritual law tells us the same thing: *Jesus Christ is the only provision for man's sin. Through him you can know and experience God's love and his plan for your life.*

And finally, Jesus made the principles personal and placed the woman in a position where she would have to make a faith decision. He revealed his identity to her, and she had to choose whether to believe. The fourth spiritual law calls for a decision based on faith in Christ: *We must individually receive Jesus Christ as Savior and Lord; then we can know and experience God's love and his plan for our lives.*

As you can see, Scripture is not written merely to give us abstract head knowledge. Its truths are practical and applicable.

Hazards to Avoid

When a golfer tees off, he or she whacks that ball straight for the pin, always hoping for a hole in one or at least to land somewhere on the green. Many hazards lie in wait to swallow the ball should it miss its mark and go astray. Water traps on one side, woods on the other, and sand traps lurk near the green.

Application in Bible study has similar hazards. If we are not alert, we can land in various traps waiting to swallow our attempts to reach our application goals. Let's identify some of these hazards.

Hazard 1: Mistaking Interpretation for Application

It's sometimes easy to think that because we have understood a truth, we have therefore applied it. We understand the principles we learned in Jesus' conversation with the Samaritan woman, and when we lodge them solidly in our mind, we can easily think we are somehow "soul winners" without ever putting the principles into practice. It's a little like a man thinking that because he wears a soldier's uniform, he is therefore a valiant warrior, though he may never have fired a shot. It's not the knowledge that counts; it's what you do with it.

Hazard 2: Procrastination

Often you may not feel like studying the Bible. That's not unusual at all. You may have spent years never bothering to study and that pattern is embedded into your lifestyle. All those years you may have been operating in the flesh and running on emotions, following the path of least resistance, and doing what your feel-good impulses told you to do. It's not easy to suddenly change those habits and begin a disciplined routine. Strong and consistent desires must be built over time, and you never get there without making a commitment and bringing your emotions under the direction of your will.

When you procrastinate, your true priorities go on display. Whenever you put off an intended action until later, you always take up some other action in its place. The replacement is your true priority.

Often you simply may not feel like studying the Bible. But what motivates me to spend time in the Scriptures is not my emotions—the way I feel—but rather my convictions. My deep belief that God speaks to me through the Bible supersedes my transient feelings.

Hazard 3: Emotional Response without Accompanying Action

You may have uncovered a profound truth that hits you hard and evokes a strong emotional response. It may be either a response of heightened joy or of godly sorrow and remorse over an uncovered sin. Yet that emotion may spend itself and fail to motivate you to action. You stop short of the goal of application and treat the emotion as an end to itself. Thus application is aborted.

Hazard 4: Expecting Instant Results

As we apply scriptural principles to our lives with prayer and dedication, it's easy to expect the result to be instantaneous. Problem solved. No more effort required. But I have learned that many times the Lord seems just as interested in the process as in the results, for it is usually in the process that we grow to be more like him. Just as work and exercise produce muscle, the process of dealing with our problems and weaknesses produces patience and faith. Instant results are rare and we should not expect them.

Hazard 5: Frustration

Frustration often grows out of expecting instant results. Frustration can also grow out of interruptions or failing to find the time you need for Bible study or thinking you are not learning all you should. Whatever the cause of your frustration, address it quickly. Lower your expectations for instant success. If you really can't find the time you desire for Bible study, use well the time you have. Don't compare your rate of learning with that of anyone else or with what you have yet to learn. Just keep on keeping on. Don't let the hazard of frustration frustrate you.

All of us occasionally land in these hazards. Even Tiger Woods' ball sometimes lands in a sand trap. The important thing is to choose the right iron and blast out again, taking more care to avoid such hazards in the future. We would like a hole in one with every tee-off, but that's not a realistic expectation. It rarely happens. Even the best golfers usually take at least three shots to reach a hole (for some of us it's seven or eight!). And it takes time and practice, practice, practice even to achieve par. The point is to stick with it. Remember that the growth process itself is important. It builds character.

A Hazard in Witnessing

I will close this chapter by addressing one hazard in witnessing that you can avoid by applying Scripture. That hazard is getting drawn into an argument with the person to whom you witness. It can happen all too easily. Their minds may be filled with trivial questions or misinformation about the Bible that come to their attention because they see you as knowledgeable. "Where did Cain get his wife?" or "Why did God have all those people in Canaan slaughtered?" are possible examples. Try to avoid chasing down such rabbit trails.

Remember that the Samaritan woman tried the same tactic on Jesus. When he pointed out that she had been married five times but was presently living with a man who was not her husband, she said, "You must be a prophet. So tell me, why is it that you Jews insist that Jerusalem is the only place of worship, while we Samaritans claim it is here at Mount Gerizim, where our ancestors worshiped?" The moment Jesus got too close to the truth about her life, she tried to deflect the direction of the conversation by starting a religious argument. But Jesus refused to be drawn in. Instead, he addressed her need to worship God in spirit and in truth.

People today are just like this woman. They try to avoid facing the moral issues in their lives and come up with questions that have been argued for ages. I seldom answer such questions when I am witnessing because they are rarely relevant and I don't want the conversation to get sidetracked into an endless argument. Instead, I usually compliment the person: "That is a good question [if it really is], and it deserves an answer. But why don't we wait until we finish the subject we're on and then

I'll give you my answer." Unless the question is very crucial or bothersome to the person, he or she will usually agree. And more often than not, by the time you finish they forget the question.

I use my judgment on these occasions, of course. If I perceive that the question really bothers the person and he or she will not track with me until I address it, I will answer it immediately. But the best course, if possible, is to avoid the sand trap of questions that may deflect you from your greater purpose. When you're witnessing, follow Christ's example. You don't want to get drawn into an argument; you just want to talk about Jesus.

Assignment

1. Choose a passage from John 3 and ask the seven application questions of it.
2. Make a thoughtful and detailed application of one truth from John 3 to your own life.

Application:
John 4, Student Sample

I. *Basic truths*
   A. John 4:27–43; People are ready to hear now: aggressive evangelism vs. friendship evangelism.
      1. Woman, vs. 29
      2. Men, vs. 39
      3. Many more men, vs. 41

II. *Application*
   A. Randoms
   B. People of other colors
   C. Coffee shops, book store, sport
   D. Free speech
      1. Freedom
      2. Problem
      3. Solutions
      4. Personal opportunity—pray-with-me invitation

III. *Changes in life*
   A. Message—direct presentation of Jesus.
   B. Share testimony more.
   C. Attitude—people are interested; God has prepared.
   D. Ask people to help me—"Give me to drink?"!!
   E. Conversation—secular to general spiritual, spiritual in general to specific.
   F. Go out of my way—break/be willing/long-standing traditions.
   G. "Message"—use Four Laws principle in developing the need/solution approach.
   H. First-encounter evangelism.

IV. *Carry out these changes*
   A. Contrast awareness.
   B. Sensitivity to Holy Spirit.
   C. Sensitivity to possible barriers.

D. Pray specifically for people in places where I am going to go.
E. Testimony written out and memorized.
F. Greater knowledge of Jesus' method of witnessing.
G. No arguing—compliment, continue.
H. Share concept with three people and in a group.
I. Holy Spirit.

V. Prayer
   A. "Lord Jesus, make me instant in season and out of season in snaring the Good News with others."

VI. Verse
   A. John 4:35.

VII. Illustration
   A. Be instant in season and out of season—*awareness of opportunities*. This chapter might be titled: "What Christ did, and what the disciples did not do (under the same circumstances)." While they were bargaining for "empanadas," Christ was leading a harlot to salvation.

   When the disciples went into town to buy some "empanadas y chorizos," who did they first pass on the way? The woman! Was she interested? Was she seeking Christ? Did the disciples talk with her? Who else did they pass? Verse 28, the men of the city! Were they interested? Did the disciples talk to them? I doubt it. They were too prejudiced at this time.

   When the disciples returned to the well, who did they pass on the way? First, the men of the city. Did they talk to them? No. Second, they passed the woman returning to the city. Did they talk to her?

   No, and they chewed Christ out for having talked to her. I wonder if the disciples would have reported what they had seen and heard about Christ (1 John 1:3) if the woman and the men would have shown interest? "While Christ brought blessing to the city, the disciples only brought business to the local stores."

Principles of Application

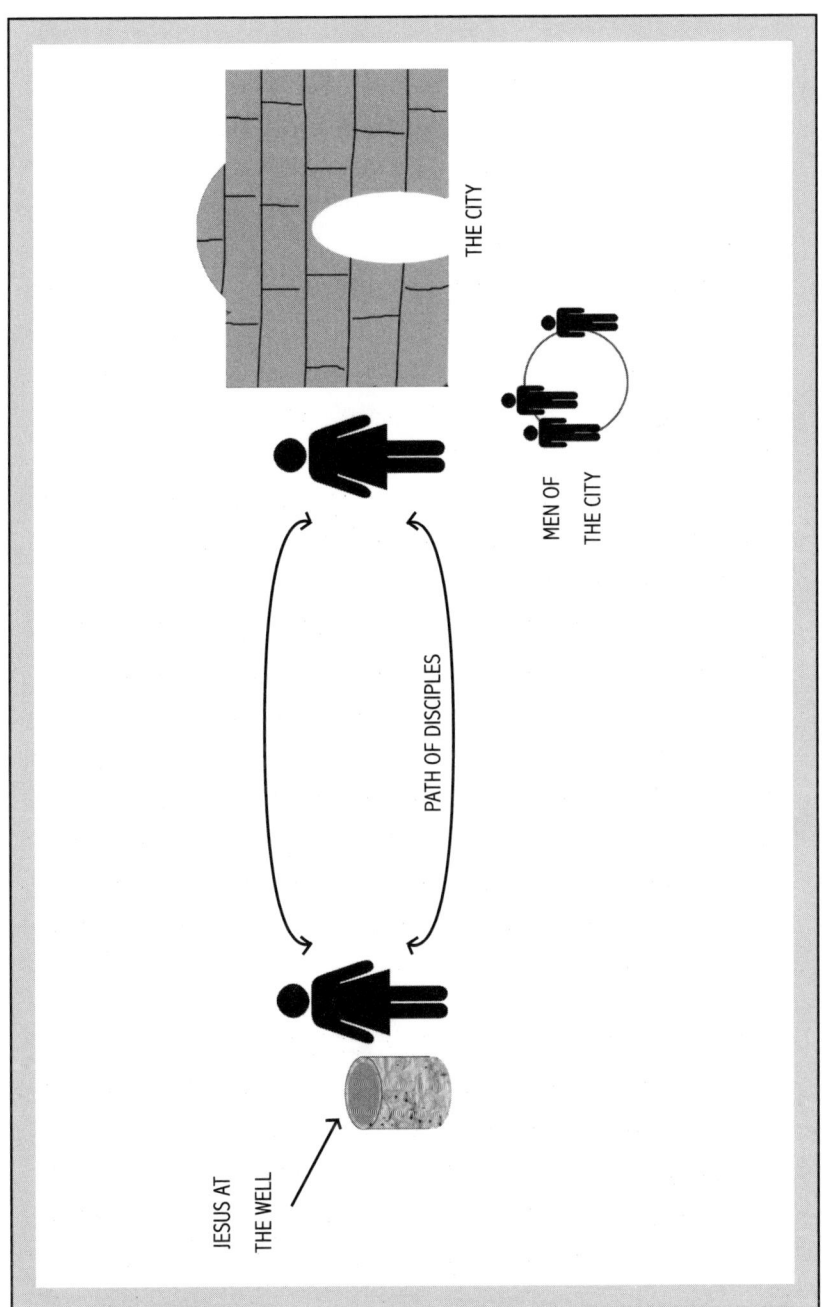

Chapter 11: Need-Driven Bible Study
Finding Answers for Your Immediate Needs

We learned in the previous chapter that the ultimate purpose of all Bible study is application. Bible knowledge means nothing unless we apply it to the way we live and use it to follow the lordship of Christ. My purpose in this book has been to lead you through an effective process of Bible study that will give you a way to gain Bible knowledge and apply it effectively.

I have found that extensive Bible knowledge is a great source of stability in one's life. The more you know, the more you can apply, and the more you apply, the more like Jesus you become, and the more like Jesus you become, the happier and more stable is your life. And we fallen humans desperately need this kind of stability. Every day we face difficulties, and often these reach the level of crises—emotional, physical, marital, vocational, or financial. We have a constant need to know God's will and see our situations from his perspective. The key is in knowing the Bible so we can apply his solutions to our needs. Our knowledge of the Bible becomes a reservoir of help for handling crisis situations.

As I've said many times before, I fully realize that the process of learning the Bible and applying its truths takes time. Extensive knowledge of God's Word will not come instantly, and meanwhile you have a life to live. What do you do when you need scriptural applications and you don't yet have the knowledge to apply? I have written this chapter as a temporary measure to help you in such cases. Think of the chapter as a tourniquet for a wound to prevent serious bleeding until your blood is built up enough to provide its own healing. Use it until you no longer need it.

First, I will show you how to find quick answers when you need them. Let's say you have a problem with your temper—a problem not all that uncommon. You have lived with your explosive outbursts of anger because they never bothered you (though those around you might have a different story). But finally your temper has created a crisis. You got angry at work and exploded in front of your boss. He called you into his office and gave you a warning, threatening termination if it ever happens again. You know you need help, and you have just begun your Bible study program. But you haven't advanced far enough to know where to find help in the Bible.

You can go to a concordance or to a word search program either online or installed on your computer. Any of these resources will give you all the passages in the Bible that deal with anger. Of course, the word "anger" appears hundreds of times in the Bible, and many of the references are to stories in which a person was angry. Others refer to the anger of God, the anger of kings, etc. For your study to be effective in dealing with your specific problem, you must narrow your search.

Next you might try a topical Bible or a Bible encyclopedia either in book form or in your computer resources and look up the word "anger." As you read the article, it will explain the several uses of the word, including a discussion of when anger is justified and when it is not. It will show you biblical warnings against anger and explain in what circumstances anger is wrong. It will also refer you to Scriptures dealing with anger in these contexts. The article will also discuss self-control as a means of harnessing anger.

Next, you can follow these references. Look up the applicable Scriptures on anger to come to a better understanding of why losing one's temper is wrong.

The mention of "self-control" in the encyclopedia article gives you another lead to follow that can get you closer to the solution to your temper problem. Read the article on self-control and again, follow through by looking up the applicable Scriptures. Write down every Scripture you find that deals specifically with your issue of anger and loss of self-control. Once you record these passages, you can apply the seven questions of the previous chapter and engage the application process you learned there.

The Crisis Bible Study Chart

Now I want to give you another resource to find help in several areas of crisis common to most of us. It is a chart containing a categorized list of scriptural references that will help you find passages that apply to your hurt or need. The fact that the Bible contains so many practical helps for our difficulties and crises is itself a tremendous faith-builder. It shows how much God cares about us and wants to minister to us in our pain. Knowing that fact is a powerful source of hope and courage.

The Scripture verses in this chart will help you to find what God has to say about your problem, frustration, or the difficult decision you must make. I am convinced that when a Christian sees what the Bible has to say, he or she finds it much easier to adjust or correct thoughts and actions that may be out of alignment with God. This is especially true of those who have hearts sensitive to God.

I pray that these helps will benefit you, that they will draw you closer to the God who loves you, and that you will find your answer in the heart of God himself.

Crisis Bible Study Reference Chart

Affection Needs — Acts 27

Alcohol and Drugs

Gen. 1:28	Rom. 13:13
Num. 6:2–4	14:21
Deut. 6:4	1 Cor. 5:11
Ps. 55:22	6:10–12
104	6:19, 20
Prov. 20:1	Gal. 5:16–21
23:20	Eph. 5:18
23:29–35	Col. 3:2
31:4–6	1 Tim. 2:5
Isa. 5:11	5:23
Matt. 11:19	1 Thes. 5:4–8
16:27–29	1 Pet. 1:13
27:34	2:13–17
Mark 15:23	4:3, 4
Luke 7:33, 34	5:7
10:34	Rev. 9:20, 21
John 2:9, 10	18:23
14:6	21:8
Rom. 12:1	22:15
13:1–5	

Anger

Ps. 2:5–9	Nah. 1:2, 3
7:11	1:6–8
10	Mark 3:5
95:11	Rom. 1:18
130:3, 4	2:5
Isa. 48:9	1 Thes. 1:10
Dan. 9:9	2:1b
Amos 5:18–20	

WARNING AGAINST HUMAN ANGER

Ps. 37:8	Prov. 22:24, 25
Prov. 10:18	24:29
14:17, 29	26:24
15:1, 18	27:5, 6
16:32	29:11, 20, 22
20:3, 22	

Need-Driven Bible Study

Anger (continued) — *WARNING AGAINST HUMAN ANGER (CONTINUED)*

Eccl. 7:9	Eph. 4:26–32
Matt. 5:22	Col. 3:8
7:1–5	2 Tim. 4:2
Luke 17:3, 4	Heb. 12:15
Rom. 12:19	James 1:19, 20
14:4	3:3–14
2 Cor. 7:8–10	4:1
Gal. 5:20	5:9

DEALING WITH IT

Gen. 4:5–7	Prov. 25:15
Prov. 15:28	Matt. 2:16
19:19	Mark 10:14
22:24, 25	John 4

EFFECTS

Ps. 73	Matt. 5:38; 44
Prov. 14:17	Eph. 4:30, 31
25:28	

Anxiety — *BAD*

Ps. 55:22	Acts 27
121	Phil. 4:6, 7
Matt. 6:25–34	1 Pet. 5:7

GOOD

2 Cor. 11:28	Phil. 2:20

"CURES"—DEALING WITH IT

John 14:1–3	Heb. 13:6
14:18, 27	James 1:22
Phil. 4:4–9	1 John 4:18

Death

Ps. 23:6	1 Cor. 15:54–58
Prov. 3:21–26	Phil. 1:21, 23
14:32	Heb. 2:14, 15

Decision Making — 2 Tim. 3:15–18   Heb. 11:23–27

Depression — [DESPAIR]

Gen. 4:6, 7	Ex. 6:9

Depression (continued)	*[DESPAIR (CONTINUED)]*	
	Num. 11:10–15	Ps. 121
	1 Kings 19	Prov. 18:14
	Job 3	Lamentations
	Ps. 23:4	Matt. 5:12
	27	11:28–30
	32	26:37, 38
	34:15–17	26:75
	38	John 4:1–3
	40:1–3	15:10, 11
	51	Acts 27
	69	Rom. 8:28
	88	15:13
	102	2 Cor. 4:8, 9
	103:13, 14	Eph. 1:3–14
	DEALING WITH IT	
	John 14:1–14	Heb. 1:3
	14:26, 27	13:5
	Col. 1:16, 17	
	PREVENTING IT	
	Phil. 4:11–13	Phil. 4:8
Desire	Gen. 3:6	Eph. 2:3
	Ex. 20:17	Titus 2:12
	Prov. 10:3, 24	3:3
	11:6	Jas. 1:13–16
	28:25	1 John 2:16
	Matt. 6:21	Jude 18
	Luke 12:31–34	1 Pet. 1:14
	Rom. 13:14	4:2, 3
	Gal. 5:16	
Discipline	Prov. 3:11, 12	1 Cor. 11:29–34
	13:24	2 Cor. 2:1–11
	19:18	12:7–10
	22:6, 15	Eph. 6:1–4
	23:13	1 Tim. 4:7
	29:15	Heb. 12:5–11
	1 Cor. 5:1–13	

Need-Driven Bible Study

Divorce	Gen. 2:18–25	Matt. 19:3–9
	Ex. 20:14	Mark 10:2–12
	Deut. 24:1–4	Rom. 6:1–2
	Isa. 50:1	12:1–2
	Jer. 3:1	13:14
	Mal. 2:16	1 Cor. 7:10–24
	Matt. 5:2	7:33–34
	5:27, 28	7:39–40
	5:31, 32	Jas. 5:16
	6:14, 15	
	CAUSES OF	
	1 Cor. 7:10–15	
	PREVENTING	
	1 Sam. 12:33	
Endurance	Ps. 40:1–3	2 Cor. 12:7–10
	John 11	Heb. 12:5–11
	Acts 27	
Envy	Titus 3:5	1 Pet. 2:1
	Jas. 3:14–16	
Fear	Gen. 3:10	Acts 27
	Ps. 103	2 Tim. 1:7
	121	Heb. 2:14, 15
	Prov. 10:24	1 Pet. 3:6
	29:25	3:13, 14
	Matt. 10:26–31	1 John 4:18
Financial	Deut. 8:11–14	Prov. 19:17
	Job 31:24–25	22:7
	31:28	23:4, 5
	Ps. 49:10–12	27:24
	52:5–7	28:20
	62:10	30:7–10
	Prov. 3:9	Eccl. 5:10
	10:9	Matt. 6:24–34
	11:1	18:23–25
	15:27	19:16–24
	17:23	25:14–30

Financial (Continued)	Mark 6:7–11 8:36 Luke 12:13–21 16:19f Rom. 13:6–8 1 Cor. 16:2	2 Cor. 8:14, 15 9:7 Phil. 4:18, 19 1 Tim. 6:7, 10 Heb. 13:5
	CAUSES OF	
	Ex. 20:17 Ps. 72:2, 3 Prov. 3:9–10 3:27–28 11:15 11:24, 25 14:21 17:18 19:15, 17 21:5 22:7	Prov. 22:26, 27 28:20, 22 Eccl. 5:15–17 Mal. 8:10 Luke 3:11 6:38 12:15–21 Rom. 18:8, 9 Gal. 6:10 1 Thes. 3:10 Rev. 3:17
	DEALING WITH	
	Gen. 1:28 Ex. 20:15, 27 Ps. 50:10–12 50:15	Ps. 55:22 Matt. 6:25–34 25:14–29 1 Pet. 5:7
Forgiveness	Ps. 32 103 Prov. 17:9 Matt. 6:14, 15 18:15–17 Mark 11:25	Luke 17:3–10 Eph. 4:32 Col. 3:13 Jas. 5:15 1 John 1:8–10
Friendship	Prov. 27:6, 10 17:9, 17	John 15:13–15
God's Love and Acceptance	Ps. 27 103	Luke 15 Acts 27
Gossip	Prov. 10:18 11:13 18:8	Prov. 20:19 26:20–22 Jas. 4:11

Need-Driven Bible Study

Grief	2 Sam. 12	Matt. 26:38
	Ps. 6:5–7	John 11
	23:4	1 Cor. 15
	119:28	2 Cor. 4:14–5:8
	137:1, 5, 6	Eph. 4:30
	Prov. 14:13	1 Thes. 4
	15:13	2 Tim. 1:10
	Matt. 5:4	Heb. 2:14, 15
	14:12–21	9:27
Guilt	Ps. 32	Luke 15
	103	Rom. 8:23
	Isa. 53:6	2 Cor. 7:8–10
	Matt. 6:12	1 Pet. 1:24
	18:21f	1 John 1:9

CAUSES

	Gen. 2:17	John 16:8, 13
	3:4, 5	Phil. 3:12–16
	3:8, 22	1 Tim. 4:2
	Job 1:9–11	1 John 1:8–10
	John 14:26	Rev. 12:10

EFFECTS

	Ps. 73	1 John 1:9
	Rom. 6:23	

DEALING WITH IT

	1 Sam. 16:7	James 5:16
	Ps. 103:14	1 Peter 3:18
	139:1–4	1 John 1:8, 9
	John 8:3–11	

PREVENTING

	Eph. 4:32	
Habit	Prov. 19:19	Gal. 5:16–21
	Isa. 1:10–17	1 Tim.
	Jer. 13:23	Heb. 5:13ff.
	22:21	1 Pet. 2:14, 19
	Rom. 6–7	

Homosexuality	Gen. 19	Rom. 1:26–32
	Lev. 18:22	1 Cor. 6:9–11
	20:13	1 Tim. 1:10
Hope	Ps. 27	Acts 27
	40:1–3	Rom. 15:4, 5
	119	1 Thes. 1:3
	121	4:13–18
	Prov. 10:28	Heb. 6:11, 18–19
	13:12	
Hopelessness, Despair	Ps. 27	Ps. 121
	40:13	John 11
	103	Acts 27
Humility	Prov. 13:34	Gal. 6:1, 2
	15:33	Eph. 5:15–21
	16:19	Phil. 2:1–11
	22:4	Jas. 4:6, 10
	29:23	1 Pet. 5:6, 7
	John 13:1–17	
Laziness	Prov. 12:24, 27	Prov. 18:9
	13:4	26:13–16
	15:19	Matt. 25:26
Life-dominating Problems	1 Cor. 6:9–12	Rev. 21:8
	21:8	22:15
	Eph. 5:18	
Loneliness	Gen. 2:18	John 11
	Ps. 25:16	Acts 27
	121	Eph. 1:3–14
	Luke 15	2 Tim. 4:9–12
	DEALING WITH IT	
	Prov. 18:24	Rom. 8:35:39
	John 3:16	1 Cor. 6:19
	Rom. 8:9	1 John 1:9
	8:14–17	4:13
	8:26–31	
Love	Prov. 10:12	Matt. 22:39, 40
	17:19	Rom. 13:10
	Matt. 5:44	1 Cor. 13

Need-Driven Bible Study

Love (Continued)	1 Pet. 1:22	1 John 5:2, 3
	1 John 4:10, 19	2 John 5, 6
Lying	Ex. 20:16	Eph. 4:25
	Prov. 12:19, 22	Col. 3:9
Marital Problems	Gen. 2:18–25	Eccl. 9:9
	Deut. 24:1–4	Matt. 5:31, 32
	Prov. 5:18	19:3–9
	8:22	1 Cor. 7:10–16
	19:13	Eph. 5:21–33
	21:9	Col. 3:18–25
	19	Heb. 13:4
	27:15, 16	1 Pet. 3:1–7
	CAUSES OF	
	1 Cor. 7:12–16	Col. 3:18–25
	2 Cor. 6:14–16	1 Pet. 3:1–7
	Eph. 5:21–33	
Marriage	Gen. 2:18, 24	1 Pet. 3:1–17
	Eph. 5:22–33	1 Tim. 3:4, 5
	Col. 3:18–21	
Parent/Child	Gen. 2:24	Eph. 6:1–4
	2 Cor. 12:14	1 Tim. 3:4, 5
Peace	Ps. 40:1–3	Rom. 5:1
	119	12:18
	121	14:19
	Prov. 3:1, 2	Phil. 4:6–9
	16:7	Col. 3:15
	John 11	Heb. 12:24
	14:27	
Pride	Prov. 8:13	Prov. 18:12
	11:2	21:24
	13:10	27:1
	16:18	29:23
Repentance	Luke 3:8–14	Acts 17:30
	24:47	26:20
	Acts 3:19	2 Cor. 7:10
	5:31	12:21
Resentment	Prov. 26:24–26	Heb. 12:15

Self-Image	Luke 15	Eph. 2:3–14
Sickness	Ps. 119:71	Luke 13:1–5
	Matt. 9:2–6	John 9:2, 3
	9:18–21	Rom. 5:3–5
	9:23V26	8:28
	10:5–8	1 Cor. 11:29, 30
	13:58	2 Cor. 2:7–10
	25:39, 40	Heb. 9:27
	Mark 6:7–13	12:22
	7:24–30	James 1:2–4
	9:20–27	5:14–1
	Luke 9:1, 2, 6	1 Pet. 1:5–7
	DEALING WITH IT	
	Rom. 11:33	James 5:6
	1 Cor. 12:25, 26	1 John 1:9
	Heb. 11:1	
Singleness	Gen. 2:18	1 Cor. 7:32–35
	Matt. 19:11, 12	Heb. 12:15, 16
	1 Cor. 7:7. 28	
Worry	Prov. 12:25	Matt. 6:24–34
	14:30	Phil. 4:6, 7
	17:22	1 Pet. 5:6, 7

Chapter 12: You Can Do It
Making Bible Study Happen

Now that we have gone through parts of the gospel of John together and learned a process for delving deeply into Scripture to learn what it says to us, I'm sure you are eager to tackle other books on your own. That eagerness is good. It will give you the momentum to get started and find a foothold for continuing. But as I have said in previous chapters, emotion is not enough to sustain you. As the novelty wears off and you get into the hard work of Bible study, that eagerness may evaporate. Then what will keep you going?

You need three things to give you the discipline and motivation to continue when you'd rather be doing something less taxing. You need a *plan*, a *priority*, and a *promise*. In this brief chapter, I will give you a little guidance in establishing all three.

A Plan for Bible Study

I've known a few compulsive people who lived every moment of their lives by a schedule and followed a plan for every activity. For one such person, you could track every oil change to his car by the chart on his garage wall. The shirts in his closet are organized by color. He has his morning routine timed to the fraction of a minute: he will finish his coffee at 7:23, have his teeth brushed by 7:29, and be backing out of the driveway at 7:33, with his trip to work timed to where he walks through the office door at precisely 7:57. I'm not one of these people. I need a keeper to know where I left my shoes last night. And I think most people are more like me than like the man on a timer described above.

But I have learned that unless you do apply some self-control and have a plan that guides and disciplines you to do what you really need to do, you won't get it done. You won't keep it up after the emotion wears off. The idea of following a rigid plan for Bible study scares off some people at the outset. But without a plan, it won't get done.

My purpose here is not to impose on anyone a specific, one-size-fits-all plan that you must build your life around. I realize that we are all different, and each of us needs a plan that will fit our own personal situation and proclivities.

The first item in the plan is to *find a regular study time.* I know people who get up at 6:00 a.m. and spend a solid hour in Bible study before they begin their day. But I know others for whom such a schedule would be a disaster. They are not morning people, and if you made them get up that early, then by mid-morning they would not even remember that they had opened their Bibles. Others may take fifteen to thirty minutes at lunch every day and then spend that much time again before turning in at night. Obviously a nurse who works the night shift will not want to study at the supposedly "spiritual hour" of 5:30 in the morning. There's nothing spiritual about ministering to sick people the next day when you can't hold your eyes open well enough to read the medicine label. You must find the right time that works for you and your situation. But the important thing is, whatever that time is, find it and stick to it.

The next facet of your plan is to determine the duration of your study. How much time will you spend at it? You may want to start with thirty minutes per day at first, then build up to an hour or more as you develop the habit of study. Your reading speed and ability to grasp the material will be a determining factor. Some people can accomplish in half an hour what another will take two hours to do. Will you study every day, seven days a week? Or perhaps five days, or six? Maybe you're a young mother with three preschool kids and you'll be lucky to get in fifteen minutes per day. That's fine. Do fifteen minutes. At first it's not the quantity or even the quality of your study time that pays off—it's the consistency. The important thing is to get into the Word regularly and spend time there. That alone will do you a world of good—or should I say, a *heaven* of good.

The Priority of Bible Study

Perhaps you've decided to get serious about Bible study but your day is already full. Your work, including travel to and from, takes nine hours. Your lunch takes one hour, and you like to spend the last half of it reading the newspaper. After all, everyone needs to stay abreast of what's going on. Then when you get home, you unwind by watching ESPN until dinner, then after dinner you and your wife have your favorite TV programs. Then there's your hobby—you're restoring a 1957 Chevy in your garage. You need that diversion after all the day's stress. Of course, you need to put in thirty minutes on the treadmill before bedtime. Then it's the news again, then you're off to bed. Looking at that schedule, you decide the best you can do is ten minutes, maybe four days each week.

Well, that's better than nothing, but what does this schedule say about your priorities? Are all these other activities really more important than your Bible study? Setting priorities shows where your heart is. I urge every Christian reading this book to be hard-nosed in examining your daily activities when you set your Bible study schedule. You may have to give up some activity or take time from one or more and give it to Bible study. It's called sacrifice, and it's one of the things Christians do.

The Promise of Bible Study

All right, I admit that this last point is not about setting your schedule—it's about the result of setting it. I want to tell you what God promises if you will be diligent about studying his Word.

Hebrews 4:12 tells us that the Bible can reveal to us our innermost desires: "For the word of God is alive and powerful. It is sharper than the sharpest two-edged sword, cutting between soul and spirit, between joint and marrow. It exposes our innermost thoughts and desires." Then in 2 Timothy 3:16, we see how understanding the Scriptures helps us control and direct those desires: "All Scripture is inspired by God and is useful to teach us what is true and to make us realize what is wrong in our lives. It corrects us when we are wrong and teaches us to do what is right." If we immerse ourselves in God's Word, he teaches us, trains us, and conforms us to the image of Christ. When the truths of the Bible become a vital part of our lives, we experience real spiritual growth. We have victory over circumstances, and watching God work in our lives brings us great joy.

You can step into Psalm 119 at almost any point and see the importance of God's Word and the blessings that come from it. As God tells us in Joshua 1:8, when we keep his Word in our minds constantly, when we meditate on his Word day and night, we will get in the habit of being obedient to him. As a result, we will be prosperous and successful—not necessarily always in material things, but his work will be accomplished in us and through us—and *that* is real success.

That is the promise of God. You can depend on it.

Appendices

Appendix A
Bonus Resources

To make *Josh McDowell's Guide to Understanding Your Bible* even more beneficial to you, we have developed a downloadable supplement entitled Bonus Resources. This free download includes blank charts you can print and fill in, study steps for easy reference, and additional samples of various charts and outlines mentioned throughout this book.

To access Bonus Resources, go to:

www.truefoundations.com/bonus

Appendix B
Paraphrasing, Topical Study, and Biographical Study

I sometimes do three additional exercises on given passages because of the specialized help they give me. I did not include these exercises within the primary text of this book because I consider them optional. I did not want to break into the sequence of the charting and outlining methods, which I think are the keys to getting a student into the Word. But I offer these exercises here for anyone who finds them beneficial.

Paraphrasing

I sometimes find paraphrasing a passage helpful in leading me into a clearer understanding of its message. Putting an idea or story into your own words forces you inside of it. The process of finding alternate words to express the thought enhances your understanding. The sample outline on paraphrasing in this appendix will guide you through the process of writing a paraphrase on a given passage.

Topical Study

At times you may need to learn what the Bible has to say on a given topic. The best approach may be to do a topical study. Our teaching examples in the body of this book were all based on passage studies, addressing whatever topics arose from them. But if you need to learn all you can on one subject, "laziness," for example, you will need to direct your study in a different way. The outline on topical study that follows will guide you in the process of studying a given subject.

Biographical Study

The third type of alternate study in this appendix is the biographical study. This is really a specialized topical study, with the subject being a person instead of a concept or idea. This third outline that follows will guide you in the process of biographical study.

The Paraphrase

Another helpful step in understanding and teaching the Scriptures is doing a paraphrase to see the details of the passage you are studying.

How to see the details of a passage by writing a paraphrase.
  A. How to paraphrase: to paraphrase a passage of Scripture is to study a passage and to restate it in your own words.
  B. How a paraphrase can help you:
    1. To paraphrase a passage requires that you think through each thought and word of the passage sufficiently enough to re-state it. It will clarify your thinking on the truths presented.
    2. It also can help your communication of those spiritual truths to others. You should seek to express the truths in terms that would be understood easily by someone else today. Put it into contemporary English. (Eugene Peterson's *The Message* is one modern paraphrase that would be good to study as an example.)
  C. How to use variety in paraphrase:
    1. A normal paraphrase: One type of paraphrase would be to take the passage one phrase at a time and rephrase it in your own words. It is important not to change just a few words in the passage but to change the entire phrase and leave almost no word the same.
    2. A condensed paraphrase: You might try to boil a passage down to perhaps two-thirds, one-half or even one-third its original length. Try not to omit the essential parts. This type is especially good for long passages or for narrative passages.
    3. An expanded paraphrase: You might expand the passage perhaps even to as much as twice its original length. You would be seeking to explain fully the meaning of the passage. It would include interpretations and explanations

of things that were not clear. This would be very appropriate for doctrinal passages rather than narrative.
4. Use of imagination: Use your imagination in paraphrasing.
   a. Sometimes try changing illustrations into modern illustrations. Instead of saying the Word of God is "sharper than any two-edged sword," you might say it is "sharper than any surgeon's scalpel."
   b. You might imagine that you are writing to some particular person today. For example, you want to paraphrase one of Paul's epistles. So, you imagine that you are writing a friend who is a new Christian, and you try to explain the truths found in the epistle to him in the language that you might normally use if you were writing him a letter.

The Topical Study

I. What is a topical study?
   A. Instead of studying a book or a portion of a book, in a topical study you are seeking to determine what is taught by Scripture on a particular subject. For example, you may wish to study what the Bible has to say about the subject "laziness."
   B. For a doctrinal study, you simply choose a doctrinal topic, such as the doctrine of justification.
   C. Because of time constraints, you may choose to limit your subject by limiting the portion of Scripture from which you obtain your material. For example: "The doctrine of Christ in Colossians," or "The use of the term *children* in the writings of John."
   D. The key to a good topical study is the selection of a good topic.

II. How to locate material for a topical study.
   A. Use a concordance. Look up the use of words which relate to your topic.
   B. Cross-references. Once you have found some passages that relate to your topic, you can often find cross-references from these to other passages.
   C. Bible dictionary. This may give you both good information and further scriptural references concerning your topic.
   D. Subject listings. Sometimes reference Bibles list Scripture references according to subject. There are also topical Bibles, such as *Nave's Topical Bible*, which write out the entire text of various passages that relate to certain topics.
   E. If you have limited your subject to a certain portion of Scripture, such as "St. Paul's prayers in his epistles," you might have to read or scan the material to locate the sections you want.

III. How to arrange the material you locate.
   A. Once you have located your material, study it and make any notes concerning things that you want to remember.
   B. Study your notes and categorize them. Group together similar ideas under similar topics. The different emphasis of the various verses will suggest various topics for the outline. As you begin to categorize verses, this may suggest to your mind further study in certain areas of the topic.
   C. Next work your material into a logical outline. Begin with a rough tentative outline and polish it as you progress. Try to fit all of your material into the outline.

IV. How to make applications from a topical study.
   See principles of application in chapter ten of *Josh McDowell's Guide to Understanding Your Bible*.

The Biographical Study
*This is really a specialized topical study—
the topic here being a person.*

I. How to research a biographical study.
   A. Things to keep in mind.
      1. You will find your material in a similar manner as you would for a topical study.
      2. Be careful if you use a Bible dictionary that you do not let it do your thinking for you or predispose your mind to certain conclusions. It may be best to read the Bible dictionary article after you have done your own thinking.
      3. Some Bible characters have more than one name, such as Saul for Paul, Cephas and Simon for Peter, Israel for Jacob. Be sure you have all the references for the person.
      4. Sometimes biblical names are used for more than one person. Saul, John, Mary, etc. Be sure that you are reading the person you want to study.
      5. Some characters have such a large portion of Scripture devoted to them that you may want to limit your study to a particular phase of that person's life. (Example: The prayer life of the apostle Paul.)
   B. Things to look for. The following suggests certain items to look for in doing a research. Sometimes, because of lack of information available on an individual, it will not be possible to find all of these things. This does not pretend to be an exhaustive list but simply a guide. You will think of other areas for study as you find information on the person being studied.

1. Background
    a. What were the circumstances surrounding his birth—when, where, etc.?
    b. Who were his parents and family? What were they like? What was their spiritual condition?
    c. How did environment and early training influence his later life?
    d. What other factors prepared him for later life?
2. Major factors of adult life.
    a. What were his major occupation and achievements in life?
    b. What was he most noted for?
    c. What people were important in his life? His friends, his enemies, his family? What influence did others have on him and vice versa?
    d. Geography—where did he live and minister?
    e. What was his relationship to God? How did this affect his life and accomplishments?
    f. Did he write any portion of Scripture? What does it show about him?
3. Major events.
    a. What were the major events of his life? What were the major crises?
    b. What were the various periods or phases of his life? What were the pivotal points which divide these periods?
    c. What was the manner, cause and effect of his death?
4. Character.
    a. What sort of character did he have?
    b. What were his strong points?
    c. What were his weak points?
    d. What were the causes and results of the strong and weak points of his character?

                e. What were his specific faults and sins? What were the consequences of this?
                f. What was his general attitude toward life and toward others?
                g. What was his spiritual status?
                h. What basic principles seemed to guide his life and his work?
        5. Influence.
                a. What effect did he have on his contemporaries?
                b. What influence did he have on subsequent history?
                c. Concerning an Old Testament character, find out the following:
                        1) Could he be considered a type of Christ? If so, in what way?
                        2) How does the New Testament represent him, if it does?
        6. Details. Do not overlook details. They add color and often prove to be very significant.

II. How to organize your material in a biographical study.
    A. You may want to arrange your material in outline form. Some of the above suggestions (B under I.) of what to look for may suggest other categories.
    B. You may want to write a character sketch of the person.
    C. Conclude your story by writing a section on suggested personal applications to your own life. These could be learned either from the positive or negative side of the life studied.

True Foundations
Living Truth for Lifelong Growth

Begin a "Christianity 101" Process

The three integrated courses described below and on the
following pages will help you reveal the heart of God
and lead your people through a spiritual formation process.

REVEALING THE **GOD OF REDEMPTION**
WHO GAVE HIS LIFE TO REDEEM US

FOR CHILDREN	FOR YOUTH	FOR ADULTS
Is Christ Really God? The Real Truth about Why Jesus Came	**Is Christ Really God?** A Personal Encounter with the Transforming Christ	**Is Christ Really God?** How to Lead your Youth to a Personal Encounter with the Transforming Christ

Uncovering the deep meaning of God's redemptive heart will open our hearts and minds to who God truly is and prompt us to commit our lives to him.
Receiving the God of Redemption leads us to live a life of:
- Faith in God
- Worship of God
- Prayer to God

REVEALING THE **GOD OF RELATIONSHIPS**
WHO GAVE HIS SPIRIT & THE WORD TO BECOME INTIMATE WITH US

FOR CHILDREN	FOR YOUTH	FOR ADULTS
Is the Bible Personally from God? The Real Truth about Living Like Jesus	**Christ Up Close & Personal** The Real Truth about God's Spirit and His Word	**Christ Up Close & Personal** How to Lead your Youth to Discover the Real Truth about God's Spirit and His Word

God gave us his Spirit and his Word to empower us to become more and more like Christ.
Embracing the God of Relationships leads us to live a life of:
- Loving Others as Christ Loves Us
- Making Godly Choices

REVEALING THE **GOD OF RESTORATION**
WHO CONQUERED DEATH & GAVE US HIS CHURCH TO RECLAIM HIS KINGDOM

FOR CHILDREN	FOR YOUTH	FOR ADULTS
Will There Really Be a Perfect World? The Real Truth about a Recreated Heaven & Earth	**Christ Will Make All Things Right** Your Mission and True Sense of Belonging in Life	**Christ Will Make All Things Right** How to Lead your Youth to Embrace Their Mission & True Sense of Belonging

God is on a mission and has given to us (his church) the same mission of reclaiming lost souls and bringing them into the family of God. *(This course is in development and will be released in 2008. Not pictured on the following pages).*
Accepting the Mission of the God of Restoration leads us to live a life of:
- Spiritual Warfare
- Spiritual Reproduction

True Foundations
Living Truth for Lifelong Growth

Revealing the **God of Redemption**
Who Gave His Life to Redeem Us

13-SESSION *ADULT* GROUP COURSE

Is Christ Really God?
This 5-part DVD series and 8-session Interactive Group Course equips adults with solid answers for who Christ really is and how to lead young people into a transformed relationship with God. The DVD series features Josh McDowell in each session and comes with a comprehensive Leaders Guide. The 8-session Interactive Group Course has a self-contained Leaders Guide with reproducible handouts for group participants. (This is a revised course previously titled *Belief Matters*.)   (Available Nov. 2006)

13-SESSION *YOUTH* GROUP COURSE

Is Christ Really God?
This youth edition 5-part DVD series combines a powerful message, compelling media illustrations, and captivating group activities to convince your students that only Christ as the true Son of God can transform our "dead lives" into a meaningful life in relationship with him. The 8-session Interactive Group Course guides them in how to live out their devotion to God, leading them to a face-to-face encounter with Christ and helping them experience a committed relationship with him. (This is a revised course previously titled *The Revolt*.)   (Available Nov. 2006)

8-SESSION *CHILDREN'S* GROUP COURSE

Is Christ Really God?
These workbooks for children grades 1-3 and 4-6 present foundational truth of Christ's deity and why he came to earth. Written in simple terms, they enable you to lead your children into a transformed relationship with Christ. The comprehensive Leaders Guide is for both the younger and older children's workbooks. Each child is to receive a workbook. (This is a revised course previously titled *True or False*.)   (Available Nov. 2006)

Living a life of faith, worship and prayer to God.
Start today at www.truefoundations.com

True Foundations
Living Truth for Lifelong Growth

Revealing the God of Relationships
Who Gave His Spirit and the Word to Become Intimate with Us

13-SESSION *ADULT* GROUP COURSE

Christ Up Close & Personal.
This 5-part DVD series and 8-session Interactive Group Course equips adults with a clear understanding of the purpose of the Holy Spirit and his Word. Sessions featuring Josh McDowell, with accompanying Leaders Guide containing reproducible handouts, leads your group to discover the key to instilling Christlike living in their young people. (Available Aug. 2006)

13-SESSION *YOUTH* GROUP COURSE

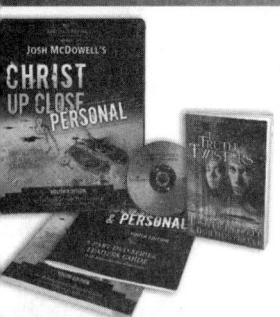

Christ Up Close & Personal.
With dynamic media illustrations and group activities, this youth edition 5-part DVD series drives home a compelling message: it is impossible to live the Christian life without the presence of the Holy Spirit and knowledge of God's Word. The 8-session Interactive Group Course leads students to love others and make right choices in the power of God's Spirit.
(Available Aug. 2006)

8-SESSION *CHILDREN'S* GROUP COURSE

Is the Bible Personally from God?
These workbooks for children grades 1-3 and 4-6 deliver a powerful message on how God's Spirit enables them to live by his Word in relationship with others. Children will learn how to yield to the Holy Spirit and how that makes both God and them very happy.
(Available Aug. 2006)

Living a life of making godly choices and loving others in Christlikeness.
Start today at www.truefoundations.com.

True Foundations
Living Truth for Lifelong Growth

Helping You to Lead This Generation through a Biblically-Based Spiritual Formation Process

ADDITIONAL RESOURCES FOR *ADULTS*

- **The Last Christian Generation** – In this book, the defining message of Josh's ministry, he offers a fresh revelation of the heart of God and 7 lifelong responses of a true follower of Christ.
- **The Relational Word** – This book reveals relationship as the true purpose of God's Word and shows how to make Christ come alive in the lives of the next generation. (Available Aug. 2006)
- **Beyond Belief to Convictions** – In this book Josh goes beyond just giving us reasons to believe; he shows how our beliefs are to be lived out in relationship with others.
- **In Search of Certainty** – We discover in this book evidence that not only is God real and truth absolute, but that trusting in him provides certainty that life has true meaning and fulfillment.

ADDITIONAL RESOURCES FOR *YOUTH*

- **The Truth Twisters** – A Novel-Plus that will captivate students with the compelling story of an entire youth group that comes face-to-face with the life changing power of the Holy Spirit and his Word. (Available Aug. 2006)
- **The Deceivers** – This Novel-Plus reveals in dramatic fashion that unless Christ is who he claimed to be—the true Son of God—then his offer to redeem us and provide meaning to life can't be real.
- **Youth Devotions 2** – This 365-daily devotional arms young people with a spiritual defense that will help them combat today's godless culture.

ADDITIONAL RESOURCES FOR *CHILDREN*

- **The Great Treasure Quest** – What is the real purpose of the Bible and who reveals its hidden secrets to us? In this easy-to-read book to children ages 7-11, unlocking the treasure of God's Word becomes an adventurous quest. They will discover how to yield to God's Spirit and obey his words. (Available Aug. 2006)
- **Children Demand a Verdict** – Children need clear and direct answers to their questions about God, the Bible, sin, death, etc. Designed for children ages 7-11, this question-and-answer book tackles 77 tough issues with clarity and relevance.
- **Family Devotions 2** – This 365-day family devotional provides younger and older children the opportunity to gather around God's Word and learn that serving him is about loving one another and allowing others to see God's love through us.

Contact your Christian supplier to obtain these resources
or **visit www.truefoundations.com.**

Other Ministries that Can Help You

INTIMATE LIFE MINISTRIES

David Ferguson and the Intimate Life Ministries (ILM) team of Austin, Texas can serve you through training and resources. They are primarily focused on providing a support network for ministers (pastors and youth workers), ministries, and Christian leaders.

ILM has developed very effective intergenerational resources, training, and seminar/training events for ministers, such as the "Galatians 6:6" and "Servant Church" retreats. To learn more visit **www.GreatCommandment.net**. For ILM's Center for Relational Care go to **www.relationalcare.org** or call 1-800-881-1808.

SONLIFE MINISTRIES

A youth worker training and church growth service focusing on fulfilling the Great Commission. Visit **www.sonlife.com**.

NATIONAL NETWORK OF YOUTH MINISTRIES

An excellent ministry to get you connected with other youth ministers in your area and gain from their experience. Visit **www.youthworkers.net**.

JESUS FOCUSED YOUTH MINISTRY

A training and resource ministry to youth workers. Visit **www.reach-out.org**.

DARE 2 SHARE MINISTRIES

A training ministry to equip Christian teens to share their faith with courage, clarity and compassion. Visit **www.dare2share.org**.

Our goal is to help you reach yours.